It is my sincere desire that the owner of this book would find within the pages healing that only comes from our loving and caring Abba-daddy!

I speak a blessing over your life that you will come to know your Abba-daddy in the full measure of his abiding mercy and power that is available to his children.

Sincerely,

Your Sister and Your Father's Daughter,

MISSION OF THE ONE HEART SERIES
To provide milk for the babe, and strong meat for the mature. To rid all who come along on this journey of religious traditions that make us white wash graves full of dead men's bones! So, that we may say as the Apostle Paul: "OH" "That I may know him, and the power of his resurrection, and the fellowship of his sufferings, being made conformable unto his death; if by any means I might attain unto the resurrection of the dead. Not as though I had already attained, either were already perfect: but I follow after, if that I may apprehend that for which also I am apprehended of Christ Jesus. Brethren I count not myself to have apprehended: but this one thing I do, forgetting those things which are behind and reaching forth unto those things which are before, I press toward the mark for the prize of the high calling of God in Christ Jesus. Let us therefore, as many as be perfect (pure in heart, italics mine), be thus minded: and if any thing ye be otherwise minded, God shall reveal even this unto you. Nevertheless, whereto we have already attained, let us walk by the same rule, and let us mind the same thing. Brethren, be followers together of me, and mark them which walks so as ye have us for an ensample. (For many walk, of which I have told you often, and now tell you even weeping, that they are the enemies of the cross of Christ: Whose end is destruction, whose God is their belly, and whose glory is their

shame, who mind earthly things.) For our conversation is in heaven; from whence also we look for the Saviour, the Lord Jesus Christ; Who shall change our vile body, that it may be fashioned like unto his glorious body, according to the working whereby he is able to even to subdue all things unto himself. (Philippians 3:10-21, KJV)

Notice is hereby given that this author claims the full trademark rights to the all inferences of the "One", the "Heart", and the name "One Heart Series" utilized throughout the various books, tapes and any and all electronic media used to convey the One Heart Series Message.

© 2012, Patricia E. Adams

TM

Copyright © 2012 by Patricia E. Adams

Printed and bound in the United States of America. All rights reserved. No part of this book may be reproduced or transmitted in any form or by any means, electronic or mechanical, including photocopying, recording, or by an information storage and retrieval system -- except by a reviewer who may quote brief passages in a review to be printed in a magazine or newspaper -- without permission in writing from the publisher. For information please contact Shekinah Publishing House, 877/538-1363. Although the author and publisher have made every effort to ensure the accuracy and completeness of information contained in this book, we assume no responsibility for errors, inaccuracies, omissions, or any inconsistency herein. Any slights of people, places, or organizations are unintentional.

Scripture quotations are from the KING JAMES VERSION of the Bible.
Printed in the United States of America

ISBN 0-9700976-2-X
LCCN 990-90787
Detouring off the Road of Oneness: From My Original Position of Oneness & Intimacy With God

---

ATTENTION ORGANIZATIONS, HEALING CENTERS, AND SCHOOLS OF SPIRITUAL DEVELOPMENT:

Quantity discounts are available on bulk purchases of this book for educational purposes. Special books or book excerpts can also be created to fit specific needs. For information, please contact Shekinah Publishing House, 1-877/538-1363.

Patricia E. Adams is a Christian, Speaker, Author, Mentor, Instructor, Coach, Leader, Children's Rights Advocate, Domestic Violence Advocate and Internet Radio Host.

She serves in her local church and community and a portion of her titles are series, one of which is called "The One Heart Series,' "The Set Free to Praise Him Series" and two upcoming series in development at this writing. She writes about the salvation journey as a process of becoming intimate with God.

There are 5 books currently in the One Heart Series; 1 in the Set Free to Praise Him Series and 4 additional titles. God has placed a strong gift of teaching within her that speaks the truth in love, with a commandment to draw his people out and into an intimate relationship with their God.

God has wrought a mighty deliverance in her life from the baggage of physical, sexual, emotional, and religious bondage. Her testimony is that God is a mighty Deliverer and Restorer. Patricia is available to share her testimony of deliverance and restoration to groups across the country and around the world.

Lectures/Seminars/Workshops/Keynotes
Writing & Publishing Seminars
Intellectual Property Workshops
Family Seminars (Men, Women and Children)
Ministry of Helps

Please contact her for additional information at
Email: author@oneheartseries.com
Radio Network: www.blogtalkradio.com/patricia-adams-live
Website: www.oneheartseries.com

This book is dedicated to My Many Mothers -
  Winnie
  Rosie M.[1]
  Marjorie
  Tommie
  Pinkie
  Verma
  Merlee
  Rosie M.

It has taken many years to realize that because I did not have my biological mother that I was missing out. Recently, one of those that I was closest to and greatly impacted by went HOME and received her reward. And it was then that I realized that I was truly blessed and to be envied that God would bless me with so many mothers, but most of all that I have been influenced by all of them. Not all of them have been kind, but God! And I won't say which ones were mean and which ones were not. Today I know that what the enemy meant for evil, God took it and turned it into my good!

---

[1] It is not a typographical error. My first mother's last name began with an "M." and the last one mentioned her name too began with an "M."

ACKNOWLEDGMENTS

First and foremost I thank my "Lord and Savior" for the life experiences and revelation of the truth of His word concerning the trials that have tried me in the fire, and to the enemies of the light of the gospel of Jesus Christ! It is because of these fiery trials and those enemies that this work was accomplished.

To my son, without your understanding and support this work would not have been possible. It is a joy and pleasure being your mother. Much loves to you my Precious!

And to God, who for many nights and early mornings called me into His presence and drew Rhema understanding of why so much pain and suffering had entered my life. He laid the solution before me, and asked me to apply it to the bitterness and pain of the aftershock of what had transpired in my life. For this there is no other that can take the place of Jesus Christ the Lover of My Soul!

We also wish to express special gratitude to the students who attended the initial Bible Study Training. Thank you for your faithfulness in drawing the Word of God out of my belly, and producing a river of living water within me. To Pastor Phillip P. Brown, Sr. and his Wife; Associate Pastor Ethel Brown, for their divine patience in allowing us to bring this material forth in a church bible study for 4 years.

A special appreciation to Pa-Pa and Mother Dear and Aunt Merlee for being there when needed the most. To Momma Tommie, Aunt Margie, Michele, Margie, and Junliah for coming alongside in their diverse ways.

Introduction

Foundation Scripture:

"And the very God of peace sanctify you wholly; and I pray God your whole spirit and soul and body be preserved blameless unto the coming of our Lord Jesus Christ. Faithful is he that calleth you, who also will do it."

(I Thessalonians 5:23)

Now unto him that is able to keep you from falling, and to present you faultless before the presence of his glory with exceeding joy. To the only wise God our Saviour, be glory and majesty, dominion and power, both now and ever. Amen.

"What is man that though art mindful of him; the Bible records. Man is a tripartite being created in the image of God as an expression of God. The divine plan of God for his created man was that he would love Him with all of himself.

This created being would have an absolute desire to fellowship with his creator; from an undivided heart.

Man was created to fulfill the purpose of God in the earth; that is to commune and glory in the benefits of God. The Word of God was the creative force that formed the heavens and the earth, and he alone holds the patent on his creation and the keys to the kingdom. Through the disobedience of one man, Adam; Satan gained legal access, permission to become the Prince of the Air, but not the Ruler of all the earth.

The Bible says that the earth is the Lords and the fullness thereof, and those that dwell within. Ownership has been Gods all alone!

A song was written that said "...What Satan said was his, has been ours all alone..."

Now, Saints Jesus Christ has completed the

work that his father sent him to do, and nothing else is required or shall be done. It is finished! Therefore, we should not allow Satan to continue to deceive ourselves into giving away our authority. If you do not give him access, he can not come in!

Jesus removed Satan's rights to entangle all areas of our lives through the plan of salvation, He restored us to our original posture in God. Yet, we perish because of a lack of knowledge of the provisions of salvation. Especially, when we protect the painful wounds and fearful memories of our lives from God's healing touch. We literally allow a legal playground to be built, played on, and ruled over by Satan and his imps.

When we receive the Holy Spirit into our hearts, he brings in the entire five-fold ministry tools to run a revival in our dead spirit. The Holy Spirit empowers us to operate as God had originally planned. He lifts us from the ashes of despair!

Ashes are used to speak figuratively in the Bible to express the total destruction of a captive city. Ashes are known to be easily scattered, perishable, and, therefore, worthless. For example, when Satan held us as sinners; we were his captive cities.

But when the Power of the Word, the Blood of Jesus and the Fire of the Holy Spirit destroyed, and stripped bare the stronghold, the threat, the penalty and the sting of sin – we were made free! When something is made it is customized to fit the owner. Those strongholds can no longer rule over us, unless we allow them to!

From that landmark of despair, God becomes our Master (Adonai), Owner and Lord. Symbolizing the authority of God and the covenant relationship from the beginning of creation until the ascension of Jesus Christ. Picture an organizational chart, and the Trinity is aligned across the Top; and in a connecting line the second row links and aligns with the first row. This is what the Trinity has done; it has included those who believe with the authority to sit in heavenly places. We are heirs, co-equals with the inheritance of Jesus. Remember the Bible records that, "The Lord said unto my Lord, "Sit thou at my right hand, until I make thine enemies thy footstool." (Psalms 110:1)

In Malachi 4:3, it says that to the Righteous, the wicked deeds of Satan are the "…ashes under the soles of our feet." Not that we are anything in ourselves, but Christ within us is our all. Jesus Christ, the Hope of Glory, Gods' Son and His Anointing took on himself our infirmities, and bore our sicknesses. If you can envision the Lamb of God as He went to Calvary! Carrying the weight and burden of mans' sinful FLESH, the stinch of disease and the full penalty of sin and it's consequences. There on the cross God laid upon Him the iniquities, and the wages of sin that had separated and broken our fellowship with God. Now as the children of God we partake of that sacrificial lamb, Jesus Christ. Jesus said that he would not drink again, of the cup; or eat of this bread of remembrance until he ascended into heaven.

He has ascended and destroyed the wage of sin, which was death! Hebrews 2:14, states that Satan's stronghold was destroyed and those who had been held in hell through fear of death who were all their lifetime subject to bondage were released. Through Jesus' death, burial, resurrection and ascension there is deliverance for us today! We have now been settled and grounded in Jesus Christ and His Anointing. As we are continuously filled with the Holy Spirit, enabled or rather empowered to remain steadfast and unmovable, like trees that are planted by the rivers of living water.

Reflection

"Just because someone did not or does not love you the way that you think they should, doesn't mean they don't love you with all they have."

We all know someone, or have known someone or persons who have not loved us as we hoped they would. Whether they were biological, or intimate, or you were victimized by both. They only gave you what they had, but now it is time to move past what they did not have to give us and give ourselves what we deserve! Freedom from carrying around the dead weight of the people who have left us feeling empty and neglected and move into position to receive love from one who can love us to the maximum capacity of what we have made room to receive. Spring (deliverance) is in the air friends, in the natural and the spirit, while we spring clean our houses, garages and offices, how about the clutter in our souls. Just by faith, not by feeling release those who have hurt you in the past and the present from a debt they can not pay, the check you are waiting to cash will bounce anyway, because remember they can not give you what they don't have. Be free in the matchless and marvelous name of the lover of your soul Jesus Christ!" Again, may you find restoration and wholeness on every page for your life!

Your Sister in His Service Until He Shouts!

Objective In: Detouring off the Road – Ps. 23

We Meditate on Psalms 23:1-2 (NLT)

It Speaks of Correction and Surrender to His leading.

1 The LORD is my shepherd; I have everything I need.
2 He lets me rest in green meadows; he leads me beside peaceful streams.
- Healing our backslidings by exploring the unsurrendered heart
- Viewing salvation in the lens of transformation as a process
- Unpeeling the fig leaves of God-hatred and self-hatred
- From the Outer Court Relationship into the Inner Court Relationship
- Spiritual Intimacy with the King of Glory

Proverbs 14:14

14 The backslider in heart shall be filled with his own ways: and a good man shall be satisfied from himself.

Luke 6:45

45 A good man out of the good treasure of his heart bringeth forth that which is good; and an evil man out of the evil treasure of his heart bringeth forth that which is evil: for of the abundance of the heart his mouth speaketh.

The healing of our wanderings and backslidings by exploring the issues of the unsurrendered heart going through the process of Salvations transformation. Gaining an understanding of God-hatred and self-hatred. We seek to unpeel the shame and self-hatred that provides layers of fig leaves to hide behind in the Outer Court Relationship and usher you into the Inner Court Relationship of Spiritual Intimacy with the King of Glory Also, I share this passage from Oswald Chambers as his insight on vision, because without a vision the people perish and often take detours. On vision Oswald Chambers, expounds on Acts 26:19 "I was not disobedient unto the heavenly vision..." He goes on to say, "If we lose the vision, we alone are responsible, and the way we lose the vision is by spiritual leakage. If we do not run our belief about God into practical issues, it is all up with the vision God has given. The only way to be obedient to the heavenly vision is to give our utmost for God's highest, and this can only be done by continually and resolutely recalling the vision. The test is the sixty seconds of every minute, and the sixty minutes of every hour, not our times of prayer and devotional meetings. "Though it tarry, wait for it." We cannot attain to a vision, we must live in the inspiration of it until it accomplishes itself. We get so practical that we forget the vision. At the beginning we saw it but did not wait for it; we rushed off into practical work, and when the vision was fulfilled, we did not see it. Waiting for the vision that tarries is the test of our loyalty to God. It is at the peril of our soul's welfare that we get caught up in practical work and miss the fulfillment of the vision. Watch God's cyclones. The only way God sows His saints is by His whirlwind. Are you going to prove an empty pod it will depend on whether or not you are actually living in the light of what you have seen? Let God fling you out, and do not go until He does. If you select your own spot, you will prove an empty pod. If God sows you, you will bring forth fruit. It is essential to practice the walk of the feet in the light of the vision."

In Volume 3 we ultimately are preparing to live as God intends for us to live as Citizens of the Kingdom. Our measurement is to portray the life that is in us as given to us by the Lord Jesus Christ! We are to learn of Him so that we may teach of Him the ways of holiness, we must accept His Love for us so that we may love as we have been loved and to be Salt and Light in the world by helping others who are in need.

Table of Contents

ACKNOWLEDGMENTS xiii
Introduction xv
Reflection xxi
Objective In: Detouring off the Road – Ps. 23 xxiii
1- Sin Lies at the Door 3
   Detour 4
   Integrity aka Congruency 24
   A Whole Heart 24
   A Tried Heart 24
   A Whole Heart in the Midst of a Perverse Nation 25
   Seeking Him with an Available Heart 26
   An Unavailable Heart 27
   The Straight Gate 28
   A Way of Escape 29
   The Main Route 30
   Lean 34
   Waver 34
   The Root of Bitterness 35
   We Needed a Savior 63
   The Sacrifice of Disobedience 69
   Recounting That Night 73
2- An Unarmed Man 85
   Purpose 85
   An Armed Man 87
   Truthfulness 88
   Breastplate of Righteousness 89
   Feet Shod 90
   Shield of Faith 91
   Helmet of Salvation 92
   Sword of the Spirit 93
   The Colicky Lust of the Flesh 94
   The Lust of the Eyes 96
3- The Seven Things 107
   He Hates - 111
   What About Satan 113
4- No Shadow or Turning 125
   Shadow 129

Deception 131
Armour of Light 132
Abdication 133
Submission 135
Surrender 136
Death 138
Burial 139
Resurrection 143
Ascension 144
Covenant 145
Ring Giver 146
Ring Maker 149
Ring Wearer 152
Reign 155

5- Detours that Delay Destiny 159
Delayed and Angry 163
Ire 164
Rage 164
Fury 165
Indignation 165
Wrath 165
Defiled 169
The Pride of Life 170
Oh That I May Know Him 171
The Commanded Blessing 175
Six Pleasures without Gods' Delight 184
Bile 185
Promiscuity 185
Associations That Weaken Your Anointing 186
Keeping Company with the Immoral 187
Keeping Company with Those Who Launch 188
Keeping Company with Idolaters & Legalist 188
Keeping Company with the Lascivious 189
Keeping Company with Those Who Sow 190
Keeping Company with Those Involved In 191
Keeping Company with Those Who Prey On 197
Excerpt from Volume I, Chapter 5 202
Seven Pleasures of Gods' Delight 205

6 – The Last Word 209
Set Your Face like Flint 210
Prelude to Promises, Prophesies & Players 213
Promises 216
Prophecies 216
Players 217
Detoured, Delayed but Still Destined 220
Gifts and Callings 224
The Conclusion of the Matter 225
Let the Redeemed of the Lord Say So 229

- 7- The Anointing of - Illegitimacy ... 239
  - Hagar ... 243
  - Gomer ... 251
- 8 – The Degradation of Sin ... 263
  - Dathan (meaning Strong) ... 265
  - Camps of Opinion ... 268
  - Authority of Faith ... 270
  - Nebuchadnezzar ... 276
  - Prodigal Son ... 277
- 9 - The Christian Who Knows the Tools ... 291
  - The Pentateuch Relationship ... 291
  - A - Genesis (In the Beginning) ... 291
  - B – Exodus (These are the names) ... 291
  - C- Leviticus (He the Lord Called Unto Moses) ... 292
  - D- Numbers (In the Wilderness) ... 292
  - E – Deuteronomy (These are the Words) ... 292
- 10- Attitude and More Attitude ... 299
  - Forbearance ... 299
  - Longsuffering ... 299
  - Meekness ... 299
  - Quietness ... 299
  - Peace ... 300
  - Patience ... 300
  - Beatitudes ... 300
  - Peacemakers ... 302
  - Sons of God ... 302
  - Matthew Chapter 5 ... 304
  - Citizens of the Kingdom ... 310
- 11- A Fly in the Ointment ... 315
  - My Dear Sisters and Brothers, ... 332
  - Defiled No More ... 334
- 12 – Be Thou Made Whole ... 343
- Endnotes ... 353
- Volumes in the One Heart Series ... 355
- Other Books by Patricia E. Adams cont'd ... 357
- Other Books by Patricia E. Adams cont'd ... 357

CHAPTER 1

Sin Lies At the Door

"...and if thou doest not well, sin lieth at the door..." Genesis 4:7

1- Sin Lies at the Door

In Hebrews 10:11-27 "And every priest standeth daily ministering and offering oftentimes the same sacrifices, which can never take away sins: But this man, after he had offered one sacrifice for sins for ever, sat down on the right hand of God; From henceforth expecting till his enemies be made his footstool. For by one offering he hath perfected for ever them that are sanctified. Whereof the Holy Ghost is also a witness to us: for after that he had said before, This is the covenant that I will make with them after those days, saith the Lord, I will put my laws into their hearts, and in their minds will I write them; And their sins and iniquities will I remember no more. Now where remission of these is, there is no more offering for sin. Having therefore, brethren, boldness to enter into the holiest by the blood of Jesus, By a new and living way, which he hath consecrated for us, through the veil, that is to say, his flesh; And having an high priest over the house of God.

Let us draw near with a true heart in full assurance of faith, having our hearts sprinkled from an evil conscience, and our bodies washed with pure water. Let us hold fast the profession of our faith without wavering; (for he is faithful that promised;) And let us consider one another to provoke unto love and to good works...for if we sin wilfully after that we have received the knowledge of the truth, there remaineth no more sacrifice for sins."

Detour

Detour is defined as being to turn aside, as a roundabout or circuitous way or course, esp. one used temporarily when the main route is closed. As you see there are many other words for detouring, but only one listed as an antonym.

The Bible says wide is the way but narrow is the gate of the way of escape.

Synonyms: angle away, angle off, arch, bow, buckle, camber, careen, circle, contort, crimp, crinkle, crook, crouch, curl, deflect, deform, detour, double, droop, flex, genuflect, hook, incline, incurvate, lean, loop, pervert, round, spiral, stoop, swerve, tilt, turn, twist, veer, verge, warp, waver, wilt, wind, yaw, zigzag

There is only one Antonym: and it is "straighten:

Matthew 7:13-14 states it plainly "Enter ye in at the strait gate: for wide is the gate, and broad is the way, that leadeth to destruction, and many there be which go in thereat: 14 Because strait is the gate, and narrow is the way, which leadeth unto life, and few there be that find it. "

Temptations, Trials and Tests

¹³ There hath no temptation taken you but such as is common to man: but God *is* faithful, who will not suffer you to be tempted above that ye are able; but will with the temptation also make a way to escape, that ye may be able to bear *it*. ¹⁴ Wherefore, my dearly beloved, flee from idolatry. 1 Cor 10:13-14 (KJV)

 God has been testing the human heart since the Garden of Eden where we were formed out of the dust of the earth for His good pleasure. In Solomon he found a man whom he could trusts his heart to build a temple, his father David was said to be a man after God's own heart; yet he was not allowed to build the temple!

 When we are tempted it is not so we fail, but that those who know our Father would rise to the occasion of victory over the temptation!

God does not tempt us, but what tempts us is what lies in our own mercenary hearts according to the secret desires and lusts of our mind, will and emotions arise the temptations!

Let's review! James 1:13-14, "Let no man say when he is tempted, I am tempted of God: for God cannot be tempted with evil, neither tempteth he any man: But every man is tempted, when he is drawn away of his own lust, and enticed." This is why sins lies at the door, and that door is your heart – sin sits there like a rabid dog foaming at the mouth at that door hoping you will want that forbidden thing so much that you are willing to risk all for the satisfaction of pursuing and conquering the object of your affection. Only to later find out that it was you that was conquered, because you are not a slave to that thing that before held nothing on you! The turnings and shadows of the heart without the application of the Word of

God is desperately wicked! The imagination of that heart is so powerful that all gates of your senses are activated to be on alert for that thing whenever it enters the room. Take note or maybe you have already, that when something or someone you find attractive to your minds eye walks in the room your senses know it before your eyes even make contact! The back of your neck begins to tighten and your respiration becomes shallow and your eyes begin to bulge and your feet begin to move and well - you know that thing I am talking about! It is wrapped in a physical body, but in reality it is the spirit of that body that is calling out to the spirit in your body for a chance encounter, maybe for the evening or maybe in that forever I do moment! But once you have obtained that satisfaction, that repeat and command performance must be re-enacted to keep your attention or else you will look for it in another or in other forms! It is a familiar spirit that seeks to be with its own kind, now if this familiar spirit has led you like James 1:14 says of the progression of that thing, 1) tempted, 2) drawn and 3) enticed. Know this that the weapon of your warfare is found above that in I Corinthians 10:13-14; if you take the way of escape and flee you will be safe! Is it really that simple? No! Let's review James 4:7, " Submit yourselves therefore to God. Resist the devil, and he will flee from you."

This is the KEY! Submission is an equal opportunity portion for male and female, and it is the submission to God that is the principal thing for the purpose of this journey! How do we submit ourselves to God? "All my bones shall declare: God, who is like You?" (Psalms 35:10). It is the heart of a man who has become a Christian that will submit to God, in this case to surrender the guidance of your life to his guidance as the full and total authority for every decision that we would make that detours us away from the path of holiness.

  WE must seek him with our whole heart, which is what David alludes to in Psalms 35:10. He says all of him will declare who is like God, because he is all in all and there is no way we will err if we follow his commands.

  Surrender is submission to to give oneself up, as into the power of another; submit or yield, ultimately to render which means to give back. Because you see we are not our own and when we live according to our own edicts we are in violatrion of the rights of the original owner. How long would you allow someone to run your house without ever consulting you to seek your approval before they made any decisions! This is what we have chosen to do when we act in this life without his authority! The one who has sacrificed so much for us and our eternal well being only ask that we allow him to lead, guide and care for us as a Pelican does for their young when feeding their beaks appear to be bloody as they retrieve food from their pouch to feed their offspring their chest looks as if they are killing themselves to give food to their young. Jesus has laid down his life for us so thar we may commune with him and be fed and nurtured by him through the act of communion. It is the body and the blood of our dear Savior that has been offered for us once and for all that has made the way of escape we speak of. Before this we were relegated to live under the weight of the law, when they placed the cross on his back this weight was symbolic of him lifting that weight off of us so that he bore our transgressions. These weighty matters that kept us dwelling on the porch of the temple and in the outer court. Every wall of separation was removed to allow us to have access; no more was his face hidden to us or his back turned to us because we were so worthy of death! This is why we surrender, we submit through the gratitude of heart for all that he has done! Many people brown nose for less than this he has given us eternal life and a way to live victoriously in whatever state we are in! No throwing ourselves away, devouring one another or taking our own lives because we feel we have no other way out! Look out for your redemption has drawn nigh to you and deliverance is in your mouth! Simply take the place of a child of the King and let him rescue your from your own ownership and repent of your sins and ask him to come into your heart and cleanse you of all unrighteousness! After this as in any ceremony comes the work of working it out! The Bible says we are to work out our soul salvation in fear and trembling! Not in terror, but in fear; acknowledgment that He is the greatest and not you! For this cause reign over our lives and the trembling comes in as the shaking takes place!

Yes, the shaking! Have you ever been looking for something and you could not find it, and you literally had to take that bag or that drawer and turn it upside down and shake out everything in order to find that one thing! Well this is the shaking and it can be messy at times, God will take the heart and shake all of the stuff that we have been loaded with from the womb and from living life on our own terms and shake it out of us in order to get to that one thing! That one thing is a heart that is so empty of selfish ambitions and soul ties and Judas Iscariot to make room for him to come in and fully occupy the space he designed for himself. There is a show or was a show called "Merge" where two people were coming together in marriage, but while they were away getting married and the honeymoon the Designer was back at their house with their separate things determining between the two whose objects best fit the life of them as a couple! And ultimately there would be discomfort in seeing their things loaded on a truck and hauled away, but when they walked into their "Merged" home they were amazed and overjoyed at how they were blended into oneness! God wants to take the detours that this life has taken you through from the womb until now and do a "Merge" create a place of "Oneness" inside of you that is satisfied to be wherever he leads you as your lifes' authority! This is Lordship! He moves from just giving you that ticket to heaven and now becomes the conductor of your journey!

Get your ticket and let's go!

I Chronicles 28:9-10 states, "9 And thou, Solomon my son, know thou the God of thy father, and serve him with a perfect heart and with a willing mind: for the LORD searcheth all hearts, and understandeth all the imaginations of the thoughts: if thou seek him, he will be found of thee; but if thou forsake him, he will cast thee off for ever. 10 Take heed now; for the LORD hath chosen thee to build an house for the sanctuary: be strong, and do it."

With the testing it is evident that there is a purpose and a plan that exceeds our human comprehension.

During this time we share together in volume 3 we want to reason with the mind until it moves out of the way and allows the spirit to respond to the heart of God! Until we reach that point in the road we must address the deceitfulness of the heart that blinds our way to answering the higher call of God! To answer this higher calling we must become congruent!

Congruent in Patricia's dictionary is when your actions line up with what comes out of your mouth. The Bible says in Luke 6:45, "A good man out of the good treasure of his heart bringeth forth that which is good; and an evil man out of the evil treasure of his heart bringeth forth that which is evil: for of the abundance of the heart his mouth speaketh."

Before we neglect to show you what you have avoided, let's take a look at what God said would happen to the children of disobedience if they chose not to heed his call! Not because he is an unloving or unmerciful God, but because there are cause and effects that govern this world, and when we transgress – break one of the cause then the effects are automatically activated! We are not punished by God, but by the effect of the choices we make, and for him to break the law for us would mean he would nullify the death, burial, resurrection and ascencion of Jesus Christ who died so that we would have a way of escape. This actually was fulfilled during the time of Hosea, because they actually disobeyed! Now in the hearing of Deuteronomy the same people who were judged and punished in Hosea were not still alive, but their descendants were. The Oral History and studying of the Torah (the Law) would have handed sufficed to remind them of what God said then and what God meant then and how near or far they were from reaping the effect of the cause (Law) they had violated.

It would be neglectful of me not to point out this passage and also, show that in Hosea this came to pass and the plan for redemption was set in place to restore us back to God. Which is the way of escape you partake of as a Christian. Let's read on in the book of Deuteronomy 28:43-68 "43 The stranger that *is* within thee shall get up above thee very high; and thou shalt come down very low. 44 He shall lend to thee, and thou shalt not lend to him: he shall be the head, and thou shalt be the tail. 45 Moreover all these curses shall come upon thee, and shall pursue thee, and overtake thee, till thou be destroyed;

because thou hearkenedst not unto the voice of the LORD thy God, to keep his commandments and his statutes which he commanded thee: ⁴⁶ And they shall be upon thee for a sign and for a wonder, and upon thy seed for ever. ⁴⁷ Because thou servedst not the LORD thy God with joyfulness, and with gladness of heart, for the abundance of all *things*; ⁴⁸ Therefore shalt thou serve thine enemies which the LORD shall send against thee, in hunger, and in thirst, and in nakedness, and in want of all *things*: and he shall put a yoke of iron upon thy neck, until he have destroyed thee. ⁴⁹ The LORD shall bring a nation against thee from far, from the end of the earth, *as swift* as the eagle flieth; a nation whose tongue thou shalt not understand; ⁵⁰ A nation of fierce countenance, which shall not regard the person of the old, nor shew favour to the young: ⁵¹ And he shall eat the fruit of thy cattle, and the fruit of thy land, until thou be destroyed: which *also* shall not leave thee *either* corn, wine, or oil, *or* the increase of thy kine, or flocks of thy sheep, until he have destroyed thee. 52 And he shall besiege thee in all thy gates, until thy high and fenced walls come down, wherein thou trustedst, throughout all thy land: and he shall besiege thee in all thy gates throughout all thy land, which the LORD thy God hath given thee. 53 And thou shalt eat the fruit of thine own body, the flesh of thy sons and of thy daughters, which the LORD thy God hath given thee, in the siege, and in the straitness, wherewith thine enemies shall distress thee: 54 *So that* the man *that is* tender among you, and very delicate, his eye shall be evil toward his brother, and toward the wife of his bosom, and toward the remnant of his children which he shall leave: 55 So that he will not give to any of them of the flesh of his children whom he shall eat: because he hath nothing left him in the siege, and in the straitness, wherewith thine enemies shall distress thee in all thy gates. 56 The tender and delicate woman among you, which would not adventure to set the sole of her foot upon the ground for delicateness and tenderness, her eye shall be evil toward the husband of her bosom, and toward her son, and toward her daughter, 57 And toward her young one that cometh out from between her feet, and toward her children which she shall bear: for she shall eat them for want of all *things* secretly in the siege and straitness, wherewith thine enemy shall distress thee in thy gates. 58 If thou wilt not observe to do all the words of this law that are written in this book, that thou mayest fear this glorious and fearful name, THE LORD THY GOD; 59 Then the LORD will make thy plagues wonderful, and the plagues of thy seed, *even* great plagues, and of long continuance, and sore sicknesses, and of long continuance. 60 Moreover he will bring upon thee all the diseases of Egypt, which thou wast afraid of; and they shall cleave unto thee.

61 Also every sickness, and every plague, which *is* not written in the book of this law, them will the LORD bring upon thee, until thou be destroyed. **62** And ye shall be left few in number, whereas ye were as the stars of heaven for multitude; because thou wouldest not obey the voice of the LORD thy God. **63** And it shall come to pass, *that* as the LORD rejoiced over you to do you good, and to multiply you; so the LORD will rejoice over you to destroy you, and to bring you to nought; and ye shall be plucked from off the land whither thou goest to possess it. **64** And the LORD shall scatter thee among all people, from the one end of the earth even unto the other; and there thou shalt serve other gods, which neither thou nor thy fathers have known, *even* wood and stone. **65** And among these nations shalt thou find no ease, neither shall the sole of thy foot have rest: but the LORD shall give thee there a trembling heart, and failing of eyes, and sorrow of mind: **66** And thy life shall hang in doubt before thee; and thou shalt fear day and night, and shalt have none assurance of thy life: **67** In the morning thou shalt say, Would God it were even! and at even thou shalt say, Would God it were morning! for the fear of thine heart wherewith thou shalt fear, and for the sight of thine eyes which thou shalt see. **68** And the LORD shall bring thee into Egypt again with ships, by the way whereof I spake unto thee, Thou shalt see it no more again: and there ye shall be sold unto your enemies for bondmen and bondwomen, and no man shall buy *you*."

 If you will read Hosea Chapter 2 at your leisure you will see that not one word of this Law failed to come to pass!

 From the heart of a desperately wicked generation came forth a deliverer that has been graciously loving towards us even we failed to love him!

It is for this reason that your backslidings and wanderings are hinderances to your walking in the fragrance of the new birth relationship!

We want to give him all of us and let him take out the worst of us and get to the best that is in us and give us an expected end of success that never fails but goes from one level of faith to the next level of faith and congruency of heart!

To obtain and attain these levels it is necessary for God to "tests" not "tempt" the human heart (1 Chr 28:9; 29:17; 32:31).

Because he made the way of escape from temptation and this is why he does not tempt us nor desire for us to tempt Him!

He is after the integrity, congruency of the heart to line up with His will for you, and His will is His Word!

Integrity aka Congruency

Origin: Latin integritas, from integer = 'intact, whole'

1. the quality of being honest and morally upright
2. the state of being whole or unified
3. soundness of construction (askoxford.com)

A Whole Heart

1 Chronicles 28:9 "And you, Solomon my son, know the God of your father, and serve him with a whole heart and with a willing mind; for the LORD searches all hearts, and understands every plan and thought. If you seek him, he will be found by you; but if you forsake him, he will cast you off for ever.

A Tried Heart

1 Chronicles 29:17-19 I know, my God, that thou triest the heart, and hast pleasure in uprightness; in the uprightness of my heart I

have freely offered all these things, and now I have seen thy people, who are present here, offering freely and joyously to thee. 18 O LORD, the God of Abraham, Isaac, and Israel, our fathers, keep for ever such purposes and thoughts in the hearts of thy people, and direct their hearts toward thee. 19 Grant to Solomon my son that with a whole heart he may keep thy commandments, thy testimonies, and thy statutes, performing all, and that he may build the palace for which I have made provision."

A Whole Heart in the Midst of a Perverse Nation

2 Chr 15:17 But the high places were not taken out of Israel. Nevertheless the heart of Asa was blameless all his days. 2 Chr 16:9 For the eyes of the LORD run to and fro throughout the whole earth, to show his might in behalf of those whose heart is blameless toward him. You have done foolishly in this; for from now on you will have wars."

2 Chr 25:2 And he did what was right in the eyes of the LORD, yet not with a blameless heart.

Seeking Him with an Available Heart

2 Chr 15:12, 15 And they entered into a covenant to seek the LORD, the God of their fathers, with all their heart and with all their soul ... And all Judah rejoiced over the oath; for they had sworn with all their heart, and had sought him with their whole desire, and he was found by them, and the LORD gave them rest round about.

2 Chr 22:9 He searched for Ahaziah, and he was captured while hiding in Samaria, and he was brought to Jehu and put to death. They buried him, for they said, "He is the grandson of Jehoshaphat, who sought the LORD with all his heart." And the house of Ahaziah had no one able to rule the kingdom. 2 Chr 31:21 And every work that he undertook in the service of the

house of God and in accordance with the law and the commandments, seeking his God, he did with all his heart, and prospered.

An Unavailable Heart

2 Chr 12:13-14 Rehoboam was forty-one years old when he began to reign, and he reigned seventeen years in Jerusalem, the city which the LORD had chosen out of all the tribes of Israel to put his name there. His mother's name was Naamah the Ammonitess. 14 And he did evil, for he did not set his heart to seek the LORD. 2 Chr 32:31 And so in the matter of the envoys of the princes of Babylon, who had been sent to him to inquire about the sign that had been done in the land, God left him to himself, in order to try him and to know all that was in his heart.

Now that we have reasoned over the deceitfulness of the heart and the consequences for the choices we make and belief that you have chosen the path that few travel on because it is a place of total surrender and relinguishment of ownership! That path will not have the room to carry a posse or a tribe or a clique but a place to carry only yourself as you go in pursuit of whom loves you and whom your soul thirsts and longs after.

The Straight Gate

What happens when we choose the straight gate; Proverbs 29:25-26: The fear of man bringeth a snare: but whoso putteth his trust in the LORD shall be safe. 26 Many seek the ruler's favour; but every man's judgment cometh from the LORD.

This is why for the purpose of this volume we want to use the root of bitterness as the primary reason why we take detours on our journey to the Kingdom of God!

A Way of Escape

1 Corinthians 10:13 (King James Version)

13There hath no temptation taken you but such as is common to man: but God is faithful, who will not suffer you to be tempted above that ye are able; but will with the temptation also make a way to escape, that ye may be able to bear it.

It is the spirit of man that houses the soul and mind of man. Yet, the spirit of God houses the things and mind of God in man. The two are at war in a one way conflict. The spirit of God is simply waiting for a flag of surrender from the spirit of man to forsake the detours and walk the path less travelled. The souls has the potential for understanding its ways, but the spirit of God the ways of God!

Take note of the alternate words for detour: [angle away, angle off, arch, bow, buckle, camber, careen, circle, contort, crimp, crinkle, crook, crouch, curl, deflect, deform, detour, double, droop, flex, genuflect, hook, incline, incurvate, lean, loop, pervert, round, spiral, stoop, swerve, tilt, turn, twist, veer, verge, warp, waver, wilt, wind, yaw, zigzag] All of them are a form of compromise or deviation from the original path or route "...esp. one used temporarily when the main route is closed..."

The Main Route

Who said the main route was closed Satan did of course, but God says a way of escape has been made for us to no longer deviate from the main course. I Corinthians 2:12a says that God's elect has not received the spirit of the world, but the Spirit of Adoption whereby we have an assurance that we have eternal salvation in response to our belief. Yet, we detour because of mental doubt or wavering which is weak in comparison to the mind of the Spirit.

When the light shines in our darkness and the Spirit removes the scales from our blinded eyes we comprehend the light and walk on the main route.

When we attempt to understand without the light we see with the mind of reasoning and intellect of the spirit of the world we do not understand the way of escape.

This spirit allows us to communicate with mankind but not comprehend the manifold counsel of God. I Corinthians 2:12b continues that we have received "...the Spirit which is of God; that we might know the things that are freely given to us of God." God has revealed to his Elect, but the eyes of the world are blind which causes them to take alternative routes other than the main route. When we become believers we see with new eyes the more excellent way laid before us!

1 Corinthians 10:21-22 (KJV) 21 Ye cannot drink the cup of the Lord, and the cup of devils: ye cannot be partakers of the Lord's table, and of the table of devils. 22 Do we provoke the Lord to jealousy are we stronger than he

When we are dangling between deciding whether to take the wide route or the straight route we are unable to drink the cup of the Lord, or eat from the Lord's Table without causing jealous indignation to rise up in the Lord! The quest is we stronger than he, and the answer is emphatically NO! Should he choose to cut us off while we are deciding whether we want to drink and eat from His Table we would be unable to fight our way out of that decision! The wide way is the place where we seek opportunity and justification for doing and being the way we are as a result of what has been done and spoken to us in our lives.

Anger (wrath), pride, thievery, cowardice and corruption lie in wait for the double-minded as God says that the thief comes to steal, kill and destroy.

Satan hopes you will chose to eat and drink from his cup and pretend to follow after God. Those are his devices and he is the master at using them to prevent us from entering into the promises of God for our lives!

Pick one, just pick any one of these synonyms to study and you will find them laden with compromise: angle away, angle off, arch, bow, buckle, camber, careen, circle, contort, crimp, crinkle, crook, crouch, curl, deflect, deform, detour, double, droop, flex, genuflect, hook, incline, incurvate, lean, loop, pervert, round, spiral, stoop, swerve, tilt, turn, twist, veer, verge, warp, waver, wilt, wind, yaw, zigzag in any dictionary and scripture searches.

Lean

Let's take lean: Proverbs 3:5-6 Trust in the LORD with all thine heart; and lean not unto thine own understanding. 6 In all thy ways acknowledge him, and he shall direct thy paths.

Waver

Let's take waver: James 4:8 says 8 Draw nigh to God, and he will draw nigh to you. Cleanse your hands, ye sinners; and purify your hearts, ye double minded. (waver) and

James 1:8 says 8 A double minded man is unstable in all his ways. (waver)

Remember we are pulling out the drawers from the Chest of Drawers!

What will come falling out before we get to that one thing?

The Root of Bitterness

"Bitterness is like cancer. It eats upon the host. But anger is like fire. It burns all clean." Maya Angelou

Bitterness is visibly manifested in everything that a bitter person is involved in from what they touch, how they speak and their lifestyle publicly and privately. Their conversation is riddled with criticism and rehashing of sour grapes, even to the point when you listen to them your countenance changes because it is hard to listen to when you are not a bitter person yourself.

Bitterness can take on the forms of various afflictions. It brings misery, bondage and leads to expressions of wickedness. A sour taste enters your mouth whenever you encounter persons or relive hurtful events. The Chaldeans were seen as a "bitter and hasty nation.

The root of bitterness can be handed down generationally and becomes a snare of danger that derails destinies.

The root of bitterness has a companion called judgment. The measure of judgment you give out to other as a result of your bitterness, becomes the judgment measured back to you; like boomerang effect. If you believe that God is in control of all things, and then this is like they say in the stunt commercials, "...don't try this at home or on your own..." Then judgment is best left in Gods' hands because he is the professional judge and knows the exacting methods of delivery to those who are in need of judgment.

Judgment stemming from the root of bitterness coming from your hands has detrimental affects to you and your generations. It leaves a blood trail, and when blood has been spilled it requires a penalty!

I highly recommend leaving it up to God! We wonder why doesn't God do something to those who have spitefully misused and abused us; and why are the people who have been good to us leaving this earth, while the wicked remain? I asked this question multiple times of God and each time I was given the same answer. Albeit the question has been asked years apart, the answer remains the same! It is simply that I would that all men would repent and be saved.

His hearts desire is that no man perishes, but it does not excuse them for the consequences of their behavior at the judgment seat. Why does it seem the people who love you sooner than the people who have harmed you? Because, sometimes we won't get out of God's way and allow him to be God!

What? The opportunity to have someone surrender to God's plan of salvation is something that all men are entitled to!

We who have been harmed would withhold that opportunity if it were left in our hands and send them straight to hell! But that is not God's way or God's heart or God's plan for man! So, why do you need to move out of the way and how do you move out of the way! Let's paint a scenario; you hear a broadcast alert that there is a storm coming of exponential proportions off the sea and it is about to touch ground and we must evacuate! You are at your house when the warning comes and you race to the attic to check and see if your prisoner is still chained to the rafters.

What do you do?

If you unchain them there is a chance they may break free and kill you for having imprisoned them. The other side of the coin is if you unchain them and take them to safety and people see you with them; because after all you told everyone that this person left town years ago and that you had not heard from them since 1926. Folks will wonder about your conflicting story. How do you keep the person from telling where they have been, you cannot gag them publicly and not go to prison yourself. So you have played this all out in your mind without ever leaving the attic, the storm is on your street now and the rescue team is at your door knocking feverishly for you to come to safety. You look at your prisoner and you look towards the door and you peer out the attic window at the storm, and you cannot make a decision.

Leave them there unchained and hope that the storm will destroy them, but there will be a body discovered after the storm is over.

Unchain them and take the chance they won't overpower you and leave you behind for dead; or you both make it out and they turn you into the police at the first opportunity.

The storm wrecks your house, the rescue team has left, are you still in the attic with the prisoner, are you dead or alive, and are they dead or alive?

What if you are both alive, you unchained and they chained; the house is totally destroyed around you and the recovery team comes by and hears movement or detects heat from two bodies.

You cannot unchain them, and the last board is about to be pulled off of the two of you and the sun is peering through blinding you.

Your secret is about to be exposed and what reasonable explanation do you have that will hold up in a court of law for your imprisonment of another individual.

We could take this scenario and go in so many other directions, but the point is you could not free yourself because you were in reality you were the prisoner too because you were chained invisibly to the one you had chained to the rafters. Or better yet were you the one chained to the rafters and your secrets were about to be exposed? Either way you were chained or chainee; neither of your could go free because of the root of bitterness! It wants revenge at all cost and it does not allow the light of reason to enter into the thought process; thus condemning you along with the criminal. When betrayals have been committed, it spawns an opportunity for bitterness through unforgiveness. It is what links the two pieces (betrayal) and (bitterness) chain links together and it has heinous consequences. Let's look at what the Bible says about the two and the affect it has on generations of people through the eyes of Hosea.

Despite what we have gone through as children or things said to us, it is the aftershocks of the trauma that drive us into other vices, situations and circumstances. Reflect back over your life of where you have been and what you want to accomplish in your life. Can't quite seem to move forward for taking two steps back sometimes!

In Hosea 7 you see a kingdom that has become divided as a result of civil war. You have the North (Israelites) and the South (Judah) and yet there is a common thread that still unites them. The common thread in this story is their family tree and an unmet need that has been handed down since King David.

The backdrop starts when one of King David's peers and a close friend made a request of the King and he declined to fulfill their request. This peer perceives this as a betrayal? Why? Because the request was within the Kings power to perform, he could have made it happen, but he didn't! That perceived or real betrayal of their friendship created a rift in their relationship that did not mend, and the friend became his enemy and became his bitter enemy. This now bitter enemy is planting the seed of discord amongst his family and friends and they being a generation of people who pass down their history orally; perpetuate the infraction of King David down through the years. And during this time small insurrections or coups would be made in an attempt to unseat the throne of David unsuccessfully.

Then the King dies, and Solomon ascends to the throne and those who were the enemies of King David are the enemies of King Solomon and the throne of David is in danger. The infighting has spawned a generation of people who want to be spoken to comfortably about their sins and the priest don't want to stop the offerings, so they cater to the desires of the people and only preach what they want to hear. Lowering the priesthood to the level of the people rather than elevating the people to the office of the priesthood! There was no distinction between the godly and the ungodly! Most of these are from the descendants of the once friend of King David with the unmet need. A rift in a relationship where one friend lets down another who had the power to grant the request and did not!

The one who made the requests goes on with life as an angry mumbler until the mumblings become audible in the hearing of those they love and influence. Their pain becomes their pain and the mere mention of the name King David is inflammatory when spoken of in their presence.

They sleep, eat, think and give birth infectiously with the hatred of David on their hearts. Perpetually they are groomed to dislike the seed of the man who denied their ancestor a favor.

Even though they look like them, and share the same blood line they want no communication and desire nothing more than an end to the throne of David. A seed was planted, becoming a crop that has wrapped its roots into the earth and refuses to be killed off until it has choked out the object of their hatred! This is a difficult root, bitterness! Have you ever seen a whole family of people who are just angry all the time?

Growing up as a little girl there was a family that lived across from us and we were told not to mess with them, they were the terror of the neighborhood and no one dared challenge them.

Well back to King Solomon the wisest man to ever live! Guess what in all of his wisdom, he has turned away from God. How could this be?

This starts with David who is the person who denies the request to his friend and this friend becomes his enemy.

He plants the seed of division in his family until the fourth generation is able to take the momentum of their generations and seize the opportunity to divide the kingdom as Solomon has weakened the throne in the eyes of the constituents who were loyal to the throne. Solomon marries a pagan, an Egyptian and taxes the people unfairly; and gives the monies to his pagan wife for spending change at the expense of the children of Israel.

He charges a tribute for people to pass through the gates to go to Jerusalem on their yearly pilgrimage. Ultimately in hopes they would soon tire of paying the tax and choose not to make the pilgrimage anymore, he wants the people to turn away from honoring God. It is bad enough that in the backdrop the enemy of his Father and the Throne are waiting for just such an opportunity to make their move!

This becomes the defining moment in the history in Hosea and that bitter blood line sees the moment they have been waiting for because the people are unhappy and they commence to sow the seeds of discord.

Heb 12:15 says "Looking diligently lest any man fail of the grace of God; lest any root of bitterness springing up trouble you, and thereby many be defiled; " It is a dangerous and destructive seed with a price attached to it remember and that is judgment. It must judge and be judged like a boomerang! It turns back on the thrower! It applies to what is in our hearts, the unknown and the unexpressed – judgment comes forth. When you exact revenge on the one you perceive who has wronged you it will not be many days before it will come back on you. It is the root of bitterness that comes back on you like food that will not digest.

The power to double back on you like the boomerang comes from the law of reciprocity which is operated by Gods law.

A tree gets its nourishment from its root system, and produces fruit after its kind! A bitter root system produces bitter fruit! I would like to recommend an additional book to read by Rick Joyner "There Were two Trees in the Garden" to be added to your library. Get the book you will see why I recommend it (smile)!

Where were we? Okay, roots drink nourishment from the soil planted in and our roots if sown into bitter soil to nourish us then our root system is cursed from generation to generation. Until you submit to the cross of Jesus Christ and allow the Blood of Jesus to drip into the soil of your heart and loosen; or as the Bible says break up the fallow ground that will allow the bitter roots to be pulled up.

As stated in Hosea 10:12 "12 Sow to yourselves in righteousness, reap in mercy; break up your fallow ground: for it is time to seek the LORD, till he come and rain righteousness upon you."

It is time for a showdown and you must confront yourself, drink and be nurtured from God, obtain mercy and be merciful. Not because you feel like it, but because it is the ways of God! Righteousness is about doing and being like God, not feeling your way through righteousness. Because feelings are whimsical and some days you feel like being righteous and other days you don't!

That is why it is not about how you feel today, if Jesus had chosen what he felt over what he knew had to be done, you and I would be dead in our trespasses with no way out! Let's examine the b clause of Hebrews 12:15 because there was a semicolon after verse 15 leading into verse 16 and 17, and it reads Hebrews 12:16 "Lest there be any fornicator, or profane person, as Esau, who for one morsel of meat sold his birthright.

17 For ye know how that afterward, when he would have inherited the blessing, he was rejected: for he found no place of repentance, though he sought it carefully with tears."

When we drink from the root of bitterness we cause further harm to ourselves on every level, and are reinforced by our sinful reactions to the things that have happened to us! How we respond to what has happened affects us not the person(s) who harmed us and therefore, it is Gods to judge and recompense the evil. Get out of the way, unchain yourself from the rafters in the attic and let that prisoner go!

We are no longer prisoners of pain and the prison guard. When God judges he is fair; but when we judge we are in turn judged. He knows how to exact vengeance on our behalf.

It is our inability to let go, meaning we refuse to forgive; because we feel entitled to hold them accountable!

Who else is going to hold them accountable if we don't, at least that is what we tell ourselves subconsciously!

The day God told me that my time was up with playing in the traffic he led me to the altar the following day and in response to a confirming word over the pulpit, I felt lifted off my seat and pushed to the altar. While standing at the altar through the power of the Holy Spirit the Pastor prayed for me in my backslidden condition to be free, I clinched my fist while he was holding my hands as if I was holding onto something for dear life and would not let go. He said you have to let go, he addressed it as unforgiveness and told me you must forgive if you are asking God to forgive you and come back into your life.

If we want to be forgiven we must do it because we cannot judge ourselves righteous, he has already done that for us through the gift of salvation.

Therefore you are illegally holding a filled office as Judge, and ultimately, it will destroy you who like it did King Saul. Remember King Saul, (See I Samuel 15:1-10) He wanted to counsel himself as Prophet as a result went into battle and did not fully obey the words from the mouth of God's Prophet Samuel who had given him instructions from the mouth of God. He disobeys and it cost him his life! The Prophet Samuel sent Saul to destroy all of Amalek and Saul does not, and God is angered at him and rejects who he had once appointed as King!

There is an appointed place and time that God has for you to be in and it is not in the place of the prison camp as the prison guard or the prisoner.

He has rolled the stone away from the grave, which is akin to him rolling away the reproach that kept you separated from God's love and the weight of sin that confined you to occupying a grave full of dead men's bones. He has called you out by name for such a time as this! This is the end of compromise and detours that drive you from his presence and into the streets!

The doors of the Church are open, come one --- come all into this Holy Place and Seek Him while he may be found!

Choose to live and walk in forgiveness as you are forgiven, 490 times a day the Bible says we are to forgive. Refusing to forgive is not an option for a life destined for fullness of joy and dancing. When we operate in unforgiveness we are enemies of God, because he sent his son for our sins and forgave us when we were enemies.

How can we crucify Jesus afresh? It is not about what has been done to us anymore, but about our response to what has been done. What are you holding out for or hoping to gain by holding onto bitterness and unforgiveness?

Feelings perpetuate victimization, we must move past feeling and getting into what we know about the Word of God, and that is that we be hearers and doers of his word!

Judgments and unmet expectations become an anchor for our validation of all that has gone wrong with us. When we look at these things as adults and triggers go off, we smack our lips as if we taste it all over again. When you encounter someone who has done you wrong, your posture and your facial expressions and the sucking of your teeth indicates you have bitterness in your life for that person.

We want justice and someone must take the blame for what has happened to this innocent child that should have been protected! But my dears it has been done, justice has been served through the death, burial, resurrection and ascension of Jesus Christ.

Hebrews 4:12-16 bears witness, "For the word of God is quick, and powerful, and sharper than any two-edged sword, piercing even to the dividing asunder of soul and spirit, and of the joints and marrow, and is a discerner of the thoughts and intents of the heart. 13 Neither is there any creature that is not manifest in his sight: but all things are naked and opened unto the eyes of him with whom we have to do.
14 Seeing then that we have a great high priest, that is passed into the heavens, Jesus the Son of God, let us hold fast our profession. 15 For we have not an high priest which cannot be touched with the feeling of our infirmities; but was in all

points tempted like as we are, yet without sin. 16 Let us therefore come boldly unto the throne of grace, that we may obtain mercy, and find grace to help in time of need."

Move out of the way and let God handle the vengeance so we can have our hands clean and holy! 1 Timothy 2:8 8 I will therefore that men pray every where, lifting up holy hands, without wrath and doubting. Remember in Volume 2 we talked about wrath; go back and review if necessary.

Reflect on this how can we lift up holy hands if we are exacting vengeance, how can we do it without wrath (anger that decries blood be spilled) and doubting (that God sees as knows all about it according to Hebrews 4:13). By what authority do we have to operate in the office as God? To maintain its posture and position in your heart it must have a focal point and that focal point is "pain".

The pain of what was done to you or by you lodged in the video library called trauma. Bitterness has a plan and that is to contaminate everything and everyone it comes into contact with, it is not static but transferable.

Let's take a look at Ruth and Naomi:

The story starts out with a wealthy man and his family living in Jerusalem during a time when most of his neighbors were in despair. Some discussions say that he grew weary of the poor coming to him for help and decided to leave Jersualem and go into the land of Moab where it was rumored to be prosperity abounding. His name was Elimelech and he dies in Moab this rumored place of prosperity. Key here is there is not a discussion with God prior to their leaving for Jerusalem if they should go to Moab recorded in the Bible, perhaps in other antiquities but not here; and for this reason we will take this position.

Remember the owner of the house who is not consulted about how to run the house? Alright then they went into what from the hearing (news broadcast of the day) that there was a place he could go with his prosperity and fit in and not be bothered with giving to the less fortunate. Ruth chapter 1, He takes his family and for a short season things are okay.

The sons are married and there are no offsprings conceived by the sons who later die as did their father. Women in those days without the headship of a man lost all status and provision for themselves.

His wife Naomi is left with daughters in place of sons who had bore no male heirs before they passed, and Naomis' womb was empty of sons! We need a man, not just any man to step in a save the day!

Naomi, prepares to return to Jerusalem and bids in Ruth 1:8, "And Naomi said unto her two daughters in law, Go, return each to her mother's house: the LORD deal kindly with you, as ye have dealt with the dead, and with me." And in Ruth 1:11, "And Naomi said, Turn again, my daughters: why will ye go with me? are there yet any more sons in my womb, that they may be your husbands? " They have arrived and Naomi is welcomed home, Ruth 1:19, "So they two went until they came to Bethlehem. And it came to pass, when they were come to Bethlehem, that all the city was moved about them, and they said, Is this Naomi?" Here you see the bitterness that has taken root in her soul come out to transfer to the crowd that welcomes her home in Ruth 1:20-21, "And she said unto them, Call me not Naomi, call me Mara: for the Almighty hath dealt very bitterly with me. 21 I went out full, and the LORD hath brought me home again empty: why then call ye me Naomi, seeing the

LORD hath testified against me, and the Almighty hath afflicted me?" Naomi changes her name to Mara (Bitter) and wants everyone to call her Bitter whenever they see her because she perceives the Almighty hath done this horrible deed to her by allowing the men to be removed from their lives!

Remember the husband did not seek permission to take his family and he placed them in the way of going against and outside of the will of God! Dare say the consequences for the cause was the effect of being disobedient! When we go through hard times we want others to relate to what we have been through and we want to be reminded of the hard times as long as we have bitterness in our hearts.

Because then we are justified of why we are bitter and we can ignore the true pain we are in and hope that one day it will end, but until it does no one should expect us to be happy again when we have had such great losses! A woman who has given birth does not expect to attend the childs funeral, let alone all of her children from her womb! What an empty feeling that must have been, she has lost her husband and all of her joy! We carry children and at the moment of labor we enter into sorrow that is later turned into rejoicing. A woman passes from life into death during that moment to give birth to life from within from the midst of the waters of the deep comes a life purposed by God! We burst into the atmosphere preprogrammed to love God if guided into this path, but for those of us who were not guided we come as strangers seeking directions to the kingdom much like in the Wizard of Oz! Just because you grew up around the church does not mean you were given the guidance needed to fulfill your purpose! Many were taught about what was unacceptable to God and not what was pleasing to God!

For this reason Proverbs 20:5 says that the "Counsel in the heart of man is like deep water; but a man of understanding will draw it out."

We are given gifts by God and Talents by God according to our abilities to complete our Purpose! Many of us use our talents aimlessly because we have not been pointed in the direction that would allow our passion to be ignited! Passion ignites when what you were born to do meets opportunity and place. When these come together you are effortlessly performing at your optimum best! Until then we struggle against the grain and are continously placed as round pegs in square holes that frustrate our purpose! Remember we needed a man to make the way clear for us from the weight of the law and inequality of purpose, and it was not any man would do time! We needed a Superhuman intervention to roll back the weighty stone from our lives and allow us to experience life as it was designed for us before the foundation of the world! Genesis 1:27 says our Purpose was as such, "So God created man in his own image, in the image of God created he him; male and female created he them. 28 And God blessed them, and God said unto them, Be fruitful, and multiply, and replenish the earth, and subdue it: and have dominion over the fish of the sea, and over the fowl of the air, and over every living thing that moveth upon the earth."

In Genesis 3:11-12 the fallen main is arraigned for the transgressions of Gods' commandment " 11 And he said, Who told thee that thou wast naked? Hast thou eaten of the tree, whereof I commanded thee that thou shouldest not eat?

We Needed a Savior

In Hebrews 10:11-27, this passage of scripture God speaks to the incapacity of man to save himself or his brethren from their sins. Even though their sacrifices were acceptable, their sins were not blotted out. He again speaks of the representative that offered one sacrifice that was more than capable of blotting out his sins and those of his brethren, and is now seated on the right hand of God, his and our Father forever making intercession for us!

The Holy Ghost our blessed comforter and paraclete stood as witness to declare that the way had been made for the covenant that would not be written on tablets of stone, but placed as tablets of flesh in our hearts and written in our minds, and our sins are remitted - paid in full forever with a perpetual credit on our account! We must enter into the new and living way that has been consecrated (set aside, and or apart for the worship or service of God) for us that allows us to draw nigh with a true heart. A true heart is one that is without guile, cunning or deception; for God searches and knows the heart, and he expects truth in our inward parts as we come to him with a sincierity that is born of perfection through Jesus Christ as in Hebrews 10:11-27.

We have been granted access into the throne of Grace, by a new and living way. The way of the Old Testament has been fulfilled through the offering of Jesus Christ as our atonement. Because of this atonement, the fear that was justly resting in Adam and Eves' heart as a result of the fall that made them reluctant to enter into his presence, has been unjustified and we are told to come boldly before the throne of Grace and in full assurance of faith, and fully persuaded that we will let nothing separate us again from he love of God! We are the sheep of his pasture and he has opened wide the door of his Holy habitation!

There is no other way, but to come in by the door that stands wide open in Heaven, (Revelations 4:1) and that is Jesus Christ! In the exodus from Egypt they were told to place the blood on the two sideposts and the upper doorpost/lintel of their homes and not the threshold of their homes. The framework that made up the door was in three parts, which can be connected to the trinity of the Godhead. Jesus was the paschal lamb that was taken into the house and sacrificed and his life sprinkled for the remission of sins. If this had not been done when the children of Israel left their homes through those doors, when the plagues and judgment were being meeted out on the Egyptians they would have been destroyed.

Remember he rains on the just and the unjust. If you notice we live in a world that is full of sin, and we are not consumed, because we have passed through the living way, the door that has been sprinkled and we are safe. Psalms 23:4, reflects the exodus for me, when the passage says, "...yea thou I walk through the valley of the shadow of death, I will fear no evil: for thou art with me; thy rod and they staff they comfort me." They walked through the death valley of Egypt safe, and into the covenant protection of God, abiding under the shadow of the Almighty. The scripture records that not one of them had their clothes, shoes or bodies to wear out!

Sin was lying at the door for them, but because they sacrificed the lamb; the plan and purpose of God; manifested. They used the promises of God in the Torah of God given from God through the mouth of the prophets. The blood of the Lamb served as an enactment of the New Testaments plan of salvation and this our Jesus has come in the fullness of time to fulfill the law. Instead of the blood of the created thing, the blood of the Creator was inside of the Lamb. When it was pierced and sacrificed; the Creators blood ran from the created body, onto the cross of the wood - the created thing; representing the earth and the fullness thereof flowing into the mouth of the earth; until the earth trembled and the sun would not shine until darkness once again covered the face of the earth. As it had in the beginning before God the Word created the Earth. Because all that had been contaminated was reclaimed and restored! The blood of God was in his veins, and the plan of salvation was executed and implemented masterfully!

Sin lies at the door friends and brethren we continue to behave as Cains' children, full of works and dead mens bones! Ignoring the only way, the true and living way leads to destruction! We want to negotiate with God on how and what we can do and what we feel compelled to give up. This is more than any of us should dare to do, yet we do it -when we enter into the sanctuary with malice, hatred, unforgiveness, bitterness, backbiting, gossip, immorality and idolatry in our hearts and attempt to lift up holy hands.

He clearly requires that we lift up holy hands without wrath or doubting, and into enter into his presence with a true heart, emptied of our agenda and ready to operate as the Holy Spirit broods over us!

We are not our own! James 1:13 "Let no man say that when he is tempted, I am tempted of God: for God cannot be tempted with evil, neither tempeth he any man."

One of my days of attempting to live my own way came with an encounter with God that I previously covered is repeated in this passage –

The Sacrifice of Disobedience

A couple of nouns for disobedience in the Greek is Apeitheia, which means the condition of being unpersuadable!

And Parakoe, meaning hearing amiss, becoming a conditional state of failing or refusing to hear!

Produces wallowing and entertainment of sin(s) that create a realm where sin can camp at your door and entangle you every move.

Some of them are guilt, sexual impurity, cults, occult, religion, spiritism, false religions, bitterness, retaliation, jealousy, rebellion, accusation, withdrawal, strife, rejection, escape, control, insecurity, passivity, depression, persecution, doubt, heaviness, mental illness, indecision, worry, schizophrenia, self-deception, nervousness, paranoia, mind-binding, sensitiveness, confusion, mind idolatry, fears (phobias & hysterias), impatience, hyper-activity, fear of authority, false burden, cursing, pride, grief, affectation, fatigue, addictive & compulsive, covetousness, infirmity, gluttony, perfection, inheritance and self-accusation.

These sins enter through our gateways; namely our eyes, ears, nose and mouth, and any orifice we yield to engage in sin with becomes a highway and a corridor to hell!

When we identify the spirit and its seed(s) we envoke the rights of restoration of Exodus 22:7! Why, because the fruit of the spirit has a counterpart and that is the work of the flesh. Each comes with its own seeds, the Bible says that every tree, fruit and seed multiplies after its kind. Remember through one mans disobdience many were defiled!

Let's examine the meaning of the seed of Adam and Eve for a moment, shall we! Cain acquisition, Abel vanity and Seth compensation. From there we have Enos man of frailty, Caanan acquisition, Mahalel God is splendor (the praise of God), Jared He that descends, Methusaleh man of the Javelin and Lamech overthrown. From Noah rest, his seed Shem renown, Ham hot or dark and Japheth persecutor. Just in that handful of names you see a pattern, that there is something in a name and a seed produces after its kind! If we were to take the time here and examine each of the lives of the individuals listed you will see that their history is colored by what their names were!

Each of them given to certain ideosyncracies and proclivities! You know ways of being and doing things! Living a life aligned with the meaning of their names.

Disobedience is like that, depending the sin you commit each comes with its own characteristics. If you sow the seed of bitterness you harvest a crop of bitterness, hatred, unforgiveness, violence, ill-temper, need for retaliation and murder. The Bible in Hebrews 12:15, says "Looking diligently lest any man fail of the grace of God; lest any root of bitterness springing up trouble you, and thereby many be defiled; and verse 16 "Lest there be any fornicator, or profane person, as Esau, who for one morsel of meat sold his birthright."

There is that word "defile" again! Disobedience defiles your temple of God and produces a harvest that further defiles many who come in contact with you. Here is this story again, because the more I think about how Gods' grace kept me in the midst of profanity and perversion to tell you this story today is humbling all over again!

Recounting That Night

Recounting this to relay that when God calls and we fail to respond we are grieving the Holy Spirit! "One night I went to a club while in a backslidden (defiled) condition, and on this particular night I encountered someone that I had fellowshipped with in church before the presence of God. He was a preacher on the run (defiled), and I a preacher in denial (defiled).

That night we found ourselves fellowshipping (defiling each other and those around us) in one of Satan's churches (a club) in the presence of Satan! If you have ever been married to God, you should be identifying with me at this point. I can tell you that there existed at that moment in time for me what seemed to be a great big finger pointing to my soul and asking me what I was doing there! Both of us were like Jonah, defiling others!

Nothing worse than being put in danger by people who are out of place, called being at the wrong place at the wrong time! Thank God for his Grace and his Mercy!

We both sat and reminisced about the light of the church of the true and living God in the darkness of the world. How the services would be so powerful and how the Lord had used us both, and we both had to admit that we knew we were out of place.

Anyone we caused to stumble that night their blood would be required of us!

That night, in that club we both seemed compelled to admonish each other to make it back to the fold before it was too late, and before Christ returned. I praise God that the last report I had of this man of God; is that he was back in the fold, and of course so am I! Thank God for his Grace and Mercy! I hope you come home real soon, maybe even today. He loves you just the way you are!

Because God never leaves us, nor forsakes us, it is we who leave God. Yet, God remains faithfully married to the backslider. Surely goodness and mercy shall follow us all the days of our lives!

If we make our beds in hell, God follows after us desiring to show himself strong on our behalf. He is not lost, it is He who finds us, at the end of ourselves.

When you have been breathed on and marked by God for himself; you can't wash him off, you can't cover him up, and you surely can't hide from Him. Once the life of God gets in you, it gets on you and marks you with a mark that screams to everybody around you they belong to Me (God)! Thank God for that identifiable covenant mark; because it is a sure signal to Satan that he can only go so far. Just like God had a hedge of protection around Job, and even when the hedge was removed, God told Satan how far he could go.

The Word of God says that in Him we live, move and have our being. God is the life, and outside of God there is death. God was on the inside of Adam working on the outside of Adam, therefore there was nothing missing, and nothing broken in or with their relationship. There was SHALOM, meaning "wholeness" in the Hebrew; no thing was broken or missing in this relationship. They experienced blessed wholeness on every level....The most fulfilling time in a Christians life is in, Acts 11:23 "...that with purpose of heart they would 'cleave' to the Lord." Order in its' pure form can not exist without God in our lives! We have a form of godliness that denies the power thereof. The word in Hebrew 'Dabaq' means to cleave, to be attached, devoted, and to hang upon. One who dabaqs' God can be built upon as a church that the gates of hell can not prevail against!"

Sin lies at the gate of disobedience! If given access it will lead you astray. If you resist it can not prevail! It can not reproduce after its kind if the seed is not planted! In this we clearly have a part to play and that is to work out our own soul salvation in fear and trembling as recorded in Philippians 2:12. Sin is in its simplest form a falling away or missing the path and becoming separated from the presence of God!

It is anything that is contrary to the will of God for our lives! We must not debate or belabor the point! Let us reason together for a moment over this word.

One night I was awakened and I was still asleep and I could hear him talking with me and see him demonstrating something to me that made my insides shake! He began by speaking of the part of Pauls letter to the Corinthians regarding offending the weaker brethren by what we do and becoming stumbling blocks. Here is the passage found in I Corinthians 8:1-13; "NOW AS touching things offered unto idols, we know that we all have knowledge. Knowledge puffeth up, but charity edifieth. And if any man think that he knoweth any thing, he knoweth nothing yet as he ought to know. But if any man love God, the same is known of him. As concerning therefore the eating of those things that are offered in sacrifice.

We are being watched by the whole earth! It is waiting on the Sons of God to manifest. Manifest what The presence of God that rules, reigns and brings rest from the reward of Satan! To show them the re-reward of God! To demonstrate the authority of a Believer whose heart is after God and empowered to work the work of him that has sent them!

Disobedience drives us from the presence of God like Adam and Eve! Thus we detour from the original plan God had for our lives for a season! During this season many of us become full of pride like Saul, Joseph, Nebuchadnezzar and Dothan led away by our own desires! Like Judas, David, Saul of Tarsus, Samuel and the Children of Israel! We see that all of these individuals suffered the consequences of disobedience, suicide, being sold into slavery, crawling like a dog, swallowed up in the earth, suicide, death and betrayal, murder, grief-stricken, and missing the Messiah! Sin pays, clearly the Bible says that the wages of sin are death! Primarily a spiritual death that is separated from the love of God!

Many years of my life have been spent on the road of being grief-stricken! When I read in Gods Word that there was a time limit on grief that he had given to the children of Israel over Moses! I was liberated down in my soul from oppressing grief! God placed before me a plan and that was to make a list of everyone that I was grieving and then every situation that I was grieving and count 30 days from that date and grieve! At the end of that thirty day period I was to let the dead bury the dead and reckon those things as dead – because I was becoming a whitewash tomb full of dead mens bones! How can you preach life and speak life if you live in the cemetery like the man of Gadarene (Luke 8:26-27)

It is the pride of life that will make you hold fast to that which is evil and abhor that which is good! It will drive you out of the presence of God! Because it is among one of the seven things God hates (a proud look) and pride goes before destruction and a haughty spirit before a fall! At the root of most falls is the spirit of pride and what are they proud of a life they desired that stopped them from seeking the face of God instead demanding the hand of God! At the entrance of thy WORD O GOD is LIGHT!

CHOOSE YOU THIS DAY WHOM YOU WILL SERVE ON PURPOSE AND WALK OUT YOUR PURPOSE!

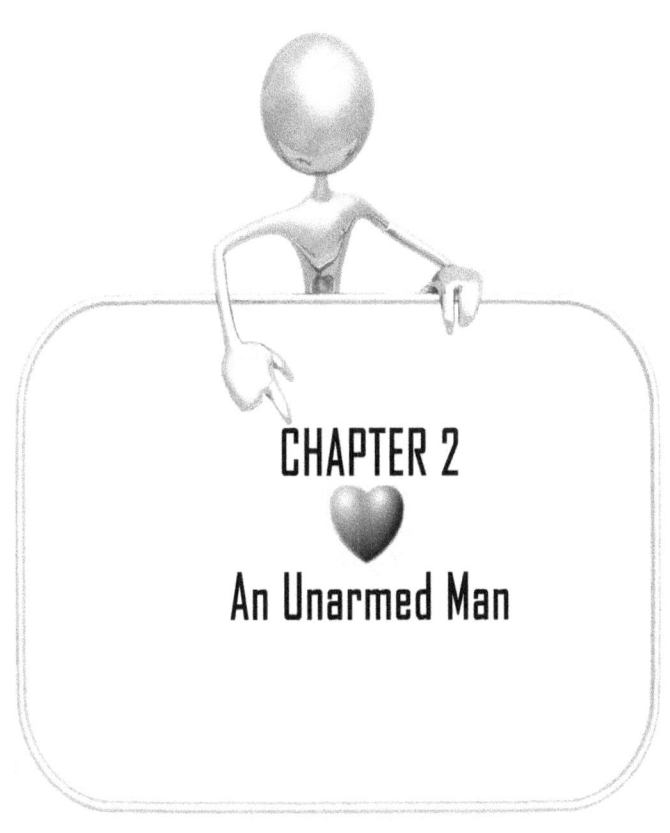

CHAPTER 2
An Unarmed Man

2- An Unarmed Man

Walking into a fight without a weapon fit for the battle you are in is suicidal! Ephesians 6, speaks of the whole armour of God; which are weapons of offense and defense. We are tossed to and fro with every wind and doctrine when we are immature, carnal and double-minded in battle times! We must be deliberate and full of purpose and that is full of God's purpose and not our own.

Purpose

Purpose, meaning one who intends to accomplish or attain an intent, design, aim, end, object, objective, or goal. Intention – implies little more than what one has in mind to do or bring about. Intent – suggests clearer formulation or greater deliberateness. Design – implies a more carefully calculated plan and carefully ordered details and sometimes scheming. Aim – adds implications of effort clearly directed toward attaining or accomplishing. End – stresses the intended effect of action often in distinction or contrast to the action or means as such. Object – may equal end but more often applies to a more individually determined wish or need. Objective – implies something tangible and immediately attainable. Goal – suggests something attained only by prolonged effort and hardship.

Imagine seeing the enemy advance on you and you are not sure which choice to make, flee, fight or surrender!

God has not given us a spirit of fear he said, but of a sound mind! And that if we would think on the things that are lovely, pure and of good report that he would keep our minds in perfect peace.

I recall ministering to a Christian who told me they did not know what peace looked like or felt like! Because their whole life had been and was presently nothing but turmoil! Shocked, I began to share with them my experience with the peace of God and asked them to take a journey with me in our minds as I described a place of peace to them! They began to weep and sense the peace but could not embrace it! Whatever you have been through up to this point in your life has been detrimental to your emotional, physical, sexual and spiritual well being. You are possibly an unarmed man or inadequately armed for the battle that you are in or are about to face up ahead!

An Armed Man

The whole armour of God follows Ephesians 6:10, 11, 13-14 10 Finally, my brethren, be strong in the Lord, and in the power of his might. 11 Put on the whole armour of God, that ye may be able

to stand against the wiles of the devil...
13 Wherefore take unto you the whole armour of God, that ye may be able to withstand in the evil day, and having done all, to stand. 14 Stand therefore, having your loins girt about with truth,

Truthfulness

In the Romans Soldiers arsenal the girdle was the key component to their ability to withstand against the adversaries they faced with full assurance they were protected. The girdle around their most sensitive and vulnerable place became the resting place for the rest of the armor. The centerpiece if you would upon which every other part was attached. The Bible says that it "Truth" in John 8:32 says that we must know the truth because it shall make us free, and in John 14:6-7 Jesus says, "...I am the way, the truth, and the life: no man cometh unto the Father, but by me. 7 If ye had known me, ye should have known my Father also: and from henceforth ye know him, and have seen him."

You SEE Jesus is THE TRUTH that our girdle represents, the whole armour of God rest on THE TRUTH "Jesus" In him we are known as we really are no deception, or shadows or turning.

A lie and a liar cannot stand up to A TRUTH from GOD THE TRUTH of GOD! Jesus is THE TRUTH, Jesus often tells us "A" Truth in the Bible, but clearly He says "I AM The TRUTH." He said to those around if that had believed that then they would know him and his father.

Breastplate of Righteousness

Guard your heart, because out of the heart flow the issues of life and death as in Proverbs 4:23 (KJV) Keep thy heart with all diligence; for out of it are the issues of life. We are the righteousness of God (the life of God) Zoe that was lost during the fall and restored to us at the obedience of God's son Jesus Christ! Again that piece of Armor points to Jesus and since we are the righteousness of God – THROUGH – Christ Jesus! When we say we are unable to live up to the standards of God's expectations for us we speak a lie, because we are being empowered by the Spirit of Truth to do and be as one who is seated on the right hand of God.

Feet Shod

Shoes on in the preparation of the gospel of peace;..." the shoes worn during times of war by the Roman soldiers were called caligas and securely fitted like an athlete laces his shoes for game time around their ankles, and the soles were impregnated with nails that gave the stability of hinds feet of a deer for balancing up the inclines and valleys allowing them to keep pace without their feet getting caught. Can you imagine fighting for your life and being unable to keep your footing Brings you peace knowing that your steps are sure; meaning you are confident in the direction you are headed and your ability to stand in the battle gives solace for those who are following you and whom you are following. Because they know your steps are ordered of the Lord and your mind is full of The Truth and your Heart is kept on and by The Truth, therefore you will not follow a lie or give faulty directions

Shield of Faith

Wherewith ye shall be able to quench all the fiery darts of the wicked..." It is custom made for you just like the other pieces of your armor. Your height and width was taken into consideration when this piece of armor was made to allow you to be fully covered as you faced the enemy. It was soaked in water to extinguish the flaming arrows that were being shot at you the moment it touched your shield.

No matter what comes at you as long as you are fully persuaded that God is for you!

Helmet of Salvation

To cover that head! I am reminded of an old church song, that said something like this. What do you know about Jesus, and the chorus He's Alright! Tell me what you know about Jesus, and the chorus He's Alright! Your mind must be persuaded and your heart fixed that you know Him and that He's Alright! They would say, well I tried him as a doctor, and the chorus would say; He's Alright, and on and on they would come up with inexhaustible ways they had tried him for themselves. They had learned to magnify God in their minds, well the helmet of salvation is like that; because affixed to the helmets top were a tall grouping of feathers that stood above the shield and the enemy had difficulty gauging exactly how tall you really were.

Proverb says, "As a Man Thinketh, So Is He." If you think you are defeated, then you are. A soldier must not allow themselves to be on the battlefield wavering (detouring) from THE TRUTH! You must KNOW THE TRUTH, and that is JESUS CHRIST!

Sword of the Spirit

which is how you come to know that he is ALRIGHT! Through studying the word of God in II Timothy 2:15, "15 Study to shew thyself approved unto God, a workman that needeth not to be ashamed, rightly dividing the word of truth." The Word of God inside of you makes you stand tall internally, so that it is projected onto the outer man and when you are fully clothed in the Armour of God you my dear friend have done nothing less than put on your robe of righteousness which is through Christ Jesus and which is none other than the Lord Jesus Christ himself!

Romans 13:14 But put ye on the Lord Jesus Christ, and make not provision for the flesh, to fulfil the lusts thereof.

The Colicky Lust of the Flesh

Flesh is like a screaming, colicky baby that has ingested air and has a distended belly and can not get any relief. Everything in the house is on edge because the child can not be appeased easily! Unbridled desires and pursuits are like a colicky baby, difficult to appease.

How do you spell relief when your flesh is colicky. Do you look for it in people, objects or thrills What would you do if you had just been denied satisfaction Would you be consolable or out of control?

How does God intend for you to reel in your flesh when you are so deeply in times where your needs scream unreasonably for relief.

The best way for me to describe this feeling – is when you know food is available and you have not made up your mind what you want to eat, but you have been thinking about eating all day and you did not eat breakfast or lunch, and now it is dinner time and the first thing you can get your hands on is what you eat, but you are not really satisfied. So, you snack and munch and eat the rest of the night. Mindful that the portion of the food you ate should have satisfied you based on the serving size. But it is something about eating what you have a desire for that does not leave you with a need for something else to satisfy you. You eat it and immediately you know to yourself that is what I have been wanting all day long! Sin to me is like that, you want sex, but you want it a certain way and with a certain person! You want to shop but you want to shop in a certain mall or store, for a certain item; you find bargains along the way that should make you stop looking for that item. But you are not satisfied because you did not obtain what your desire was set on! You have gone from your thought life to your eye gate and engaged every one of your senses in seeking satisfaction only to discover that it is temporary gratification. It takes more of the same thing to get the same feeling! You never get to feel that fleeting feeling again quite the same way! Now our eyes are full of darkness! And if your eye be full of darkness then so is your whole body!

The Lust of the Eyes

Self-denial blinds and darkens the window of the eye of the soul. The eyes are said to be the window to the soul. When the eyes are dark the view is affected inward and outwardly.

Being full of darkness pretending to be enlightened, but these are the light is dim. There are spirits that manifest in the pupil of the eyes when the body is full of darkness or shadows of turning are present. My experience with the visibility of these spirits is worth noting because they are deceptive. When a person whose under the influence of the spirits walk by and looked back as a glance their eyes literally have an orbital range that appears as if their eyes are looking backward. Your eyes lock on theirs and your breath is captivated and adrenalin races and what you see must be oppressed or possessed of the enemy. A person tormented by a lascivious spirit appearance in their eyes can sometimes be similar to a ravenous animal. Lasciviousness has entered in and caused them to have uncontrollable urges makes them predatory! The hunt for prey is on and the hunt for what will satisfy this voracious appetite! This spirit devours without getting satisfaction; and must increase the quest for fulfillment. It becomes obsessed with self and roams to and fro like Satan looking for whom they may devour!

The lust of the eyes looks at the things which are seen and become stimulated to the point of obsession over an outwardly attractive person, and once we take the wrapper off and play with it a little while; the beast appears and then it is too late to withdraw! There are beautiful people who are beautiful through and through and there is nothing wrong with that! But when your number one criteria is to seek after the flesh of that person and not their spirit, you are asking for a double dose of misery.

Satan perverts and blinds us with the secret desires of our hearts. When a woman's husband leaves for another woman less attractive or less sophisticated and accomplished than she is. She becomes highly offended, her pride is wounded and more than anything it creates a large void deep within her that makes her question her own beauty; and thus she becomes subconsciously insecure.

Creating an opening for one to become obsessed with the worlds way of doing and being. After all the world infers that beauty is not fleeting or fading with all the means presented to keep a youthful appearance.

The spirt of God moved, brooded over the face of the deep that was without form or void and drew from within that void to himself and drew out the beauty that was concealed or hidden in what seemed useless. The pride of life will cause you to look to the world for remedies and potions and procedures to maintain, or attempt to hold onto what has been diminished through inappropriate usage. Excessiveness and gluttony of life as in Luke 7:34 and Proverbs 23:20

This scorned woman wonders and exclaims to anyone who will listen, 'what does he see in her? What she has failed to realize the less attractive woman may have spent more time seeking the face of God and allowing him to display her inner beauty, and thus on display is a certain confidence outwardly that makes her a more attractive counterpart. What is on the inside of a person will show up on the outside, sooner or later.

David said in Psalms 37:31 that this man, who has the law of his God in his heart; will see none of his steps slide. I believe we can even believe that God would be our greatest potion and remedy along with proper care of ourselves not allow us to slide in our faces or extremities. After all he is the manufacturer!

 Jeremiah said in Chapter 32:39, "...that those who do these things will be his people, and he their God, and I will give them one heart, and one way, that they may fear me forever, for the good of them, and of their children after them...I will put my fear in their hearts, that they shall not depart from me...yea, I will rejoice over them to do them good, and I will plant them in this land assuredly with my whole heart and with my whole soul." We have a form of godliness that denies the power thereof. The word in Hebrew 'Dabaq' means to cleave, to be attached, devoted, and to hang upon. One who dabaqs' God can be built upon as a church that the gates of hell can not prevail against!

If we will be willing and obedient we will eat the good of the land! Then the Lord shall command the blessing upon thee in thy storehouses, and in all that thou settest thine hand unto; and he shall bless thee in the land which the Lord thy God giveth thee...if that thou hearken unto the commandments of the Lord thy God, which I command thee this day, to observe and to do them: And thou shalt not go aside from any of the words which I command thee this day, to the right hand, or to the left, to go after other gods to serve them."

Remember the patterned life of one who accepts, receives, and applies the divine order for his life is the righteous man who follows these steps:

"BLESSED IS the man that walketh not in the counsel of the ungodly, nor standeth in the way of sinners, nor sitteth in the seat of the scornful. But his delight is in the law of the Lord; and in his law doth he meditate day and night. And he shall be like a tree planted by the rivers of water, that bringeth forth his fruit in his season; his leaf also shall not wither; and whatsoever he doeth shall prosper...

BUT ...

the ungodly are not so: but are like the chaff which the wind driveth away. Therefore the ungodly shall not stand in the judgment, nor sinners in the congregation of the righteous.

For the Lord knoweth the way of the righteous; but the way of the ungodly shall perish."

A blessed man is an obedient man. That man is like a tree planted by the rivers of water. That man is not a sinner (oops) but a righteous man. One who practices the way of God and walks therein. The whole conclusion of God's purpose for our lives!

Everything else is the outworking of the in-working of Deuteronomy 28 and Psalms 1. Your calling and election are manifestations of your inward walk of righteousness, and the method by which God chooses to express your inward walk. Such as Apostle, Prophet, Teacher, Evangelist, or Pastor.

The ability to operate with ease in these comes from the fruit of the spirit, which is the outward flow of your love walk.

The love of God is shed abroad from breast to breast! The gifts of the spirit operate like a gauge on a car measuring the amount of gas in your car. The effectiveness of your gifts are a direct relationship to the measure of anointing in your life. In Deuteronomy 6:5 "Love the Lord your God with all your heart, and all your soul, and with all your strength." Instead we seek to gain our life, and ultimately we lose it!

CHAPTER 3

The Seven Things

3- The Seven Things

...Thy pomp is brought down to the grave, and the noise of thy viols, the worm is spread under thee, and the worms cover thee. How art thou fallen from heaven, O Lucifer, son of the morning! how art thou cut down to the ground, which didst weaken the nations!

Why! Because thou hast said in thine heart...

- I will ascend into heaven,
- I will exalt my throne above the stars (the angels) of God:
- I will sit also upon the mount of the congregation, in the sides of the north;
- I will ascend above the heights of the clouds:
- I will be like the most High (take God's place).

Yet thou shalt be brought down to hell, to the sides of the pit. They that see thee shall be brought down to hell, to the sides of the pit."(Christians) have focused on what Satan is doing and not on what Satan can not do! We give him credit where there is no credit due him, where things are out of order in our lives, we need look no further than the mirror! I am speaking of free will choices, not choices that were made or forced on us!

Don't get angry, get free of the bondage that you have created by being led away by your own desires and lust! James 1:14 –15 says "But each one is tempted when he is drawn away by his own desires and enticed. Then, when desire has conceived, it gives birth to sin; and sin, when it is full-grown, brings forth death."

The number nine (9) is the number of the Holy Spirit, of completeness, finality, and fulness. There are 9 Gifts and most have been taught that there are nine (9) Fruits; including myself. After further study and understanding that there is only one (1) fruit with a nine-fold expression. Much like you would see an orange or a pomegranate has sections, but is only one fruit!

Which further explains the presence of pomegranates between each bell on the hem of the High Priest garments. We have one seed sown in the womb of a woman and 9 months for the expression to manifest outwardly! Even in twin births they begin as one then splits!

Satan tries to woo us into captivity as evidenced in Jeremiah 29:30, 31; and to accomplish this Satan appeals to the soulish desires of man, his self-centered motives and aspirations for control.

He appeals to mans' fallen nature of this will for self-preservation, self-fulfillment and boisterous self-grandisement.

Satan and his minions lie in wait for our souls at the gate of every door available to us to trick and manipulate us into contaminating our temples!

Spiritual contamination of polluting the Body of Christ that is you, because you are the church also known as the Body. God is coming back for an overcoming church, those whose robes have been washed in the blood of the lamb! Yet, God speaks to the heart of mans' issues and self-afflictions to teach us how to use our own dominion and power; also known as authority.

Clearly in Proverbs 6:16-19, it states that "These six things doth the Lord hate: yea, seven are an abomination unto him that are a part of Satan's arsenal.

We have had the choices of others imposed on us and we have made our choices based on those choices.

Now it is time to grow in the wisdom of God and undo some of those choices that were detrimental!

He Hates -

A Proud Look

Uplifted eyes and high-minded actions that perceives oneself as greater than the rest of their associates or humankind.

A Lying Tongue

A lying Tongue hates the truth and has no desire to speak the truth.

Hands that Shed Innocent Blood

Hands that waste the blood of others who have not committed injustices against them or others are guilty of murder or brutalities.

A Heart that Deviseth Wicked Imaginations

Is a heart that plots the down-fall of others by lying, planting and building evil and malicious thoughts in their minds and others that create scandals and destruction.

Feet that be Swift in Running to Mischief

Have you ever seen people that will run to the scene of a fight or crime quickly trying to be the first to witness what is happening and quickly observe the scene and begin sensationalizing the details. They can hardly wait to go tell their version of what happened regardless to having missed the beginning of the turn of events.

He Hates - A False Witness that Speaketh Lies

This one is self-explanatory because they are incapable of speaking of the truth even under oath.

He that Soweth Discord (Abomination)

"To his soul." They trouble – trouble! Because they are so full of mischief and vain imaginations that peace escapes them. Wherever they are or go disruptions occur leaving behind stress and chaos among people. Destroying families,, friends, associates, churches, and anyone who eats their lies and misrepresentations. Wickedness that binds and twist the mind by wicked thoughts and actions towards brethren like wicker "twisted".

What About Satan

"Isaiah 14:4,9,10-15 "That thou shalt take up this proverb against the king of Babylon, and say, How hath the oppressor ceased! The golden city ceased!...Hell from beneath is moved for thee to meet thee at thy coming: it stirreth up the dead for thee, even all the chief ones of the earth; it hath raised up from their thrones all the kings of the nations. All they shall speak and say unto thee, Art thou also become weak as we art thou become like unto us Thy pomp is brought down to the grave, and the noise of thy viols, the worm is spread under thee, and the worms cover thee. How art thou fallen from heaven, O Lucifer, son of the morning! how art thou cut down to the ground, which didst weaken the nations!

Why! Because thou hast said in thine heart…

- I will ascend into heaven,
- I will exalt my throne above the stars (the angels) of God:
- I will sit also upon the mount of the congregation, in the sides of the north;
- I will ascend above the heights of the clouds:
- I will be like the most High (take God's place).

Yet thou shalt be brought down to hell, to the sides of the pit. They that see thee shall be brought down to hell, to the sides of the pit."…(Christians) have focused on what Satan is doing and not on what Satan can not do! We give him credit where there is no credit due him, where things are out of order in our lives, we need look no further than the mirror!

I am speaking of free will choices, not choices that were made or forced on us!

The one who gives power to all of us, gave him his power and devices to him. The power given to Satan by God is real, but not greater than the power God has given his people. We even falsely accuse Satan of being at the root of our failures. Don't get angry, get free of the bondage that you have created by being led away by your own desires and lust! James 1:14 –15 says "But each one is tempted when he is drawn away by his own desires and enticed. Then, when desire has conceived, it gives birth to sin; and sin, when it is full-grown, brings forth death." The bottom line is that Satan's destiny is defined in Ezekiel 28:12-19 and Revelation 12:7,10,12. Ezekiel 28:12-19(NKJV) reads "Son of man, take up your lamentation for the king of Tyre, and say to him, 'Thus says the Lord God:

"You were the seal of perfection, Full of wisdom and perfect in beauty...You were in Eden, the garden of God; Every precious stone was your covering:

The sardius, topaz, and diamond, beryl, onyx, and jasper, sapphire, turquoise, and emerald with gold. The workmanship of your timbrels and pipes was prepared for you on the day you were created. "You were the anointed cherub who covers; I established you; you were on the holy mountain of God; …You walked back and forth in the midst of the fiery stones. You were perfect in your ways from the day you were created. Till iniquity was found in you.

By the abundance of your trading You became filled with violence within, And you sinned; …Therefore I cast you as a profane thing Out of the mountain of God; And I destroyed you, O covering cherub, From the midst of the fiery stones. Your heart was lifted up because of your beauty; You corrupted your wisdom for the sake of your splendor; I cast you to the ground, I laid you before kings, That they might gaze at you.

You defiled your sanctuaries by the multitude of your iniquities, By the iniquity of your trading; Therefore I brought fire from your midst; It devoured you, And I turned you to ashes upon the earth In the sight of all who saw you. All who knew you among the peoples are astonished at you; You have become a horror, And shall be no more forever."

Lucifer received from God at the moment of his creation: a name that meant shining one, Seal of Perfection, full of Wisdom, perfect in Beauty, covered in Nine Stones and Gold. Again we see the number five (5) a symbol of God's grace.

The number nine (9) is the number of the Holy Spirit, of completeness, finality, and fulness. There are 9 Gifts, 9 Fruits, and 9 months for the "Fruit of the Womb." Timbrels (internal tambourine like drum) and Pipes (flutes or other woodwinds) with every breath he praised God, an Anointing to Cover, Established, and enabled to walk in the midst of the Fiery Stones and a Free Will.

So let's play role reversal with what Lucifer had. First his name is now Satan meaning opposer and adversary of both believer and unbeliever – nobody's friend, the seal of imperfection, full of foolishness, perfectly ugly, non-precious stones (fakes), tarnished brass, removal from the trinity and given a number assignment of six (6), representing man and not God, a beast, unfinished (suppose this is why God will finish him), and full of emptiness, instruments that condemn instead of praise, unable to praise God – can only speak curses on himself, others and to God with every breath, an anointing to uncover – point the finger (accuser of the brethren), and unable to walk in the midst of the fiery stones, but consumed by the fire.

Satan lost his free will and became subject to the children of God in the earth, and many of us don't know or act like it. Some of us are catching on, hurry, did you catch up?

I believe it is that way, and in another time and place I would love to prove it to you. For now think about it and study it for yourself!

When Adam yielded his purpose to Satan, the whole earth and all that was within the earth fell out of the divine order of God. As a result of the fall, Satan becomes god of this world (Genesis 3:11, 22-23) and Adam transferred his dominion of this world over to Satan (Genesis 3:4-5).

From that point until the Ascension of Christ, man strives for success and fulfillment that eludes him and brings fleeting pleasure (Genesis 4:3-8).

The children of man are born divided and saddled with the seed of strife and murder in their hearts (Genesis 4:9). The woman seeks to fill her void without relief with temporal things, baubles and beads. All of mankind and the earth were filled with a longing for "unity and restoration" (Genesis 4:16).

The loss of eternal life in Genesis 3:19,22 demanded a cry for a savior, and a response from a redeemer.

Satan was already on the earth dwelling in total darkness, when God came to create on the earth form and fullness. Satan had been on board left to devise weapons of assault on the earth.

In an effort to stop all of mankind from returning back to communion with God in Paradise, Satan tries to woo us into captivity. (Jeremiah 29:30:, 31)

To accomplish this Satan appeals to the soulish desires of man, his self-centered motives and aspirations for control. He appeals to mans' fallen nature of the will for self-preservation, self-fulfillment and boisterous attitudes.

Ultimately his aim is to destroy God's creation by weakening the kingdom of God through wars, pestilence, hunger, plagues, homicides, murders (abortions), suicide, genocide, immorality, accusations of the Saints, and lawlessness. He uses money as the central dividing line, and the pursuit of attaining money to separate the people from one another.

These are the steps and how they develop in mans' life. First, there is the love of money. Then apostasy through the unbridled desire to have the pleasures of the earth as ones' own...."

Satan and his minions lie in wait for our souls at the gate of every door available to us to trick and maninpulate us into contaminating our temples and thus polluting the Body of Christ as a whole. We are told to let the wheat and the tare grow together, and we are also told that He is coming back for an overcoming church, those whose robes have been washed in the blood of the lamb! Yet, God speaks to the heart of mans' calamities and self-afflictions and of all of them He has given us dominion and power. Clearly in Proverbs 6:16-19, it states that "These six things doth the Lord hate: yea, seven are an abomination unto him:

CHAPTER 4

This Requires No Shadow or Turning

4- No Shadow or Turning

Hebrews 12:15, 22 and 27.

"Looking diligently lest any man fall of the grace of God; lest any root of bitterness springing up trouble you, and thereby many be defiled...But ye are come unto mount Zion, and unto the city of the living God, the heavenly Jerusalem, and to an innumerable company of angels...And this word, Yet once more, signifieth the removing of those things that are shaken, as of things that are made, that those things which cannot be shaken may remain."

and James 1:17 through 21

"Every good gift and every perfect gift is from above, and cometh down from the Father of lights, with whom is no variableness, neither shadow or turning. Of his own will begat he us with the word of truth, that we should be a kind of firstfruits of his creatures..Wherefore my beloved brethren, let every man be swift to hear, slow to speak, slow to wrath: For the wrath of man worketh not the righteousness of God. Wherefore lay apart all filthiness and superfluity of naughtiness, and receive with meekness the engrafted word, which is able to save your souls."

"In Genesis Chapter 3, Adam and Eve became imperfect. Full of darkness and the absence of light and Adam for the first time in his life saw himself as a failure!

Eve loses direct communication with God as an equal to Adam. Both of their desires change toward God and each other. Eve loses her place of refuge in Adam as his closest advisor, so they begin to say you just don't understand me. Deception was born into the heart of mankind through the seed Satan planted in them! Since the time of the fall a wide door throughout the ages has been opened to divide relationships on every level through the deeds of deception! Instead of selflessness we now have self-centeredness. All of this occurred and more because of what happened in Genesis 3:2-6. They touched the forbidden tree of good and evil in the midst, the center of the Garden of Eden, which was the key to abundant life. Which is also connected to the Tithe. The tree possessed the element of blessing as long as Adam and Eve were obedient, everything in the Garden focused in the center – because it represented God's commandment......Proverbs 7:1-3, says "MY SON, keep my words, and lay up my commandments with thee. Keep my commandments, and live, and my law as the apple of thine eye. Bind them upon they fingers, write them upon the table of thine heart."...

 The penalty of the law was given when God told Adam and Eve to not eat of the forbidden tree, this was the seal of Government in the Garden of

Eden...once the seal of the law was broken, lawlessness spread throughout the entire creation....a curse comes upon the lawless. God does not have to curse anything or anybody, simply violate the law that is governing that part of the universe and you reap the curse. I have set before you life and death, blessings and cursing – choose life, God said. Malachi 3:6-13,18 references the blessing and the cursing. The center of man's existence is dependent on his desires towards God...

Adam robbed God, cursed his seed and his house, and birthed the spirit of conflict into the world's system (Satan's domain, Genesis 3:3).

Within our desires towards God lies a struggle of selfishness versus self-sacrifice. Before the fall we were fixed on communion with our CREATOR! Since the fall we have dimmed the lights on the line of communication.

It has been said that our eyes are the window to our souls. Windows serve a two-fold purpose, to see others and to be seen. God looks through the window of our eyes to see into our souls! What does he see when he looks through your windows Selah - pause and think about it!

Shadow

Have you ever seen a lamp that is lit and a sheer cover with a tint of color in it lay over the lamp thus creating an ambience of softness to the room It changes the brightness of the light and the mood of the room changes, so it is with mankind - our mood and/or countenance changes when the shadows of the works of the flesh are displayed. It is like a shadow that passes in front of you and blocks out the light and the environment is charged with the presence of darkness.

This is in essence the shadow that comes up before the candle of God (the Holy Spirit) inside of a Christian. There is a change in the color of a person and the brightness of their countenance when shadow(s) exist within them. This signifies that duplicity in nature is at war with the spirit of God. It is the spirit of God that wills to do good in and through us. When we refuse to walk in the divine nature of God and walk after the flesh a shadowing occurs that is visibly discernable by the Holy Spirit. For this reason we must know those that labor among us. Be not deceived God is not mocked whatever a man soweth that shall he also reap! Deception is rampant in the world! Even in the Body of Christ! The Bible records that if it be possible even the very elect will be deceived. Discernment! Discernment! Discernment!

Discernment come forth in the sons of God for such a time in the Kingdom of God, in Jesus Name. Amen! We must be like the sons of Issachar during this hour!

Deception

The ability to take a measure of truth and cloak it in a series of lies.

When we are no longer deceived by ulterior motives and selfish ambition, but fully intent on doing only the will of the Master. We are vessels of honor fit to be used in the Kingdom of God, as long as your kingdom exist there is the presence of the root of deception that produces Shadows and Turning!

Hebrews 12:15, 22 and 27.

"Looking diligently lest any man fall of the grace of God; lest any root of bitterness springing up trouble you, and thereby many be defiled...But ye are come unto mount Zion, and unto the city of the living God, the heavenly Jerusalem, and to an innumerable company of angels...And this word, Yet once more, signifieth the removing of those things that are shaken, as of things that are made, that those things which cannot be shaken may remain."

... and James 1:17 through 21

Armour of Light

Romans 13:11-14 says to us twelve commands of how we are to conduct ourselves before God! "And that, knowing the time, that now it is high time to awake out of sleep: for now is our salvation nearer than when we believed.

The night is far spent, the day is at hand: let us therefore cast off the works of darkness, and let us put on the armour of light. (bold mine) Let us walk honestly, as in the day not in rioting and drunkenness, Not in chambering, and wantonnness (quarreling), not in strife and envying (jealousies) But put ye on the Lord Jesus Christ, and make not provision for the flesh, to fulfill the lusts thereof. Somebody has to rule and somebody has to reign and somebody has to serve!

Abdication

Many of us have abdicated the throne room in exchange for the pig pen. We have relinquished and surrendered our royal ring, robe, crest and power for things we were never predestined to have. Because of this we find ourselves wandering like vagabonds with no permanent home or place of sanctuary!

The worst choice any human can make is to live his life without God on board! Detours cause delays, but thanks be unto God they don't have to become denials! Gifts and callings are without repentance!

And we have a high priest who is making intercession for us! But how long shall we stand halted between two opinions! If God be God then serve God! Choose you this day whom you will serve!

If you are detoured and delayed, I pray you will get back on track so your delay does not become a denial. Remember many will call upon the name of the Lord, and he will ask who they are and politely tell them I know you not!

Is your name about to be blotted out where it matters most!

You can be on the guest list of Governors, Presidents, CEO and Charities and miss being on the family roll call of Heaven!

Exchange ownership of your life through submission to the rightful owner, who is none other than Your Creator - God!

Submission

Is not slavery or bondage, but recognition of the spirit of God within us as our authority or owner! Submitting to God first means we commit totally to his directives and his authority over us! When someone who has authority meets another who is in authority they will acquiesce to the one who has the most authority by locale and region. They are not submitting to the person who holds the office but the office aka position that person occupies. When we encounter God it should be obvious who has the authority in that meeting place! We know that all authority has been given by God and he allows one man to be put up and another put down, because God has ordained the office and this is what we submit to. Such offices as Parent, Husband, Wife, Pastor and Governing officials are offices ordained by God! It does not require your liking the person occupying the office but loving the God who ordained the office! The office is the vehicle of their authority and getting their job completed is all that is of any consequence while holding that office! When we view submission this way it no longer becomes male or female, Black or White, Likes You or Doesn't Like You! We surrender to Gods' will so that it may go well with us according to the blessings of Deuteronomy.

Surrender

Give up your rights to control your world to God! We own nothing that will be taken with us on the eternal exit. It all belongs to God and he is lending us the vessel (our bodies) its' contents and all the accumulated wealth temporarily for His good pleasure! The earth is the Lord's and the fullness thereof!

We are stewards as the Bible speaks of the vineyard and the vine dressers stating that each is worthy of their hire, no matter what time they started to work!

The wage is set, seems unjust! It is not like you reported to work late in the day and received pay, but you reported as soon as you were hired to do the work measured out to you and for that you were offered a wage equal to one who had started earlier. Grace is in operation in the passage of the laborers in the vineyard, because many are falling away and the last shall be first! We like the idea of possessing and owning, and all we are doing is putting to the exchange what belongs to God!

When we make a quality decision to let go and do it God's way always! We must acknowledge that God knows whats best and the final outcome is known by him! Doesn't mean we agree 100% but we acknowledge that he knows better than we do and we are mere specks of dust, with at best a three pound brain attempting to dictate to the mind of God who is the brain creator! We must become his and allow him to become ours! He said that he would be our God and we would be his people! Through reconciliation and the spirit of adoption we are endued with power. Givien joint authority; heirship to reign, to rule and to rest in the Kingdom of God through the Death, Burial, Resurrection and Ascension of Jesus Christ!

Death

We have died to ourselve and no longer behaving as a dictator telling the brain maker how to run our lives. We no longer have to pay the penalty of sin; which was eternal death, because we had a substitute stand in for us on our day of reckoning! The death penalty was not thrown out but completed through Jesus Christ! We are not dying as Jesus died a physical death that was the penalty for sin! He obeyed in our place completely so we would only have to die a spiritual death through receiving the gift of salvation purchased by his death on the cross!

We submit our flesh to the power of the Holy Spirit to reign over our flesh in dominion by the authority of the Holy Spirit to Gods' will! Which is the Word of God! We become clothed in righteousness when we pass through death through submission, exchanging your will for God will because it is our reasonable service! After all we were released from the debtors prison!

Burial

Placing your will under the blood of Jesus and relinquishing the existence of self-willed living in exchange for a surrendered way of living. Everything about us is placed in the soil of the Word of God. We die inside of that soil as seed dies under the crushing power of the death packed upon it! The shell it crushed, the outer man as the Word of God says must die daily! Until the blade of the new life is able to overcome the hard outer shell and push its way up through the dirt that was once its grave! When it springs out from beneath the dirt it has gained authority over that dirt! My God! Oh grave where is your victory and death where is your sting.

He got up from the dirt that was stacked on him for us and it can no longer hold us down! Can you imagine going to the cemetery and laying down next to an occupied grave to tell the grave attendant to pour dirt on you because you are dead. Clearly dead men don't talk to the grave attendants!

How foolish that would be for the attendant to say, okay and begin pouring dirt on top of you as you lay on top of the ground! Because it would be illegal for him to dig a hole and bury you alive; he would be guilty of murder! This is what we are doing when we lay down and act as if we have no hope; surely – surely!

Get up from there, no matter what you have been through you cannot legally occupy a grave anymore until it is your time! You can hasten the day of your reburial, but look there is really no reason to die an eternal death through suicide. When you have the right to eternal life! You are miserable here on earth you believe, from what the Bible says you will be really miserable spending eternity in hell! Allow the Word of God to wash, transform, renew your way of thinking by accepting him not just as your Savior, but also as your Lord. You can be saved and not allow Jesus to be the Lord of your life. Have your ticket punched to get on board and everything and just take a your position when he comes back and just be glad you are going to heaven! Or you can stay right here and bring heaven down to this earthly existence you dread so much! Paul teaches us how to abase and abound, and with whatever time you have left down here you should want to really cause Satan and his imps some discomfiting!

He hates our praise and worship of God! He hates for us to realize that God is greater than anything we are going through and in turn magnify him above the circumstances! He hates the fact that you get to live where he can never live again! He hates us when we become the Sons of God, because he knows what we are entitled to as Sons!

Satan is a liar, a deceiver and destroyer of all that God has meant for good in your life! He comes to steal, kill and destroy and he is 100% committed to his purpose, and that is to keep you from being 100% committed to your purpose! Come on get up and wash your face, hands and feet! Anoint yourself and put on the Lord Jesus Christ! We are the Sons of the Most High God by Position and not Gender! He makes us hate who we are and leads us into self-mutilation of our bodies as a way of hurting

God! How can the clay say to the potter why have you made me like this! He made you for his good pleasure in His image!

If something genetically has affected your life don't blame it on God, Satan is the one who seeks to pervert all that God creates. God is not a dictator, and sometimes defects occur due to various reasons that exist in the earth, but the original plan of man was not flawed! Because God said everything he made was good and very good! When Adam saw his rib manifest in front of his eyes beyond his wildest expectation he did not identify with himself or a clone of himself but a part of himself that would enable him to fulfill purpose; be fruitful and multiply, subdue and have dominion as God instructed!

Resurrection

The seed of salvation is crushed and the blade comes forth and springs forth into a new life. It sheds the hard shell that confined the mystery of life and causes us to spring forth united to God as heirs and joint heirs of his only begotten son so that we may take not just any seat, but our rightful seat, wear our righteous attire; no more fig leaves and to be in our righteous minds – let this mind be in you which was in Christ Jesus!

Being about his Fathers Business Ruling, Reigning, Subduing and Multiplying in Purpose!

Ascension

We are seated with Jesus Christ as joint heirs in heavenly places because when he ascended we were granted access to ascend too, after he poured out his spirit on all flesh in Acts. Jesus sealed the redemption of man forever in heaven and transferred us from the penalty of death into the promise of everlasting life and that being the Zoe life – the God life we were intended to have. Jesus sealed the redemption. Jesus said Father prepare me a body and I will redeem man back to you! Here we are now empowered to be sons and daughters of obedience and recipients of covenant promises! Engrafted into the family of the Abrahamic Covenant

Covenant

This covenant was written in the flesh of Jesus through his many wounds, stripes and crown of thorns. Seventy-two (72) crowns for the nations pierced his head and thirty-nine (39) stripes bore on his body for the diseases of man, and five (5) wounds in his flesh to move us out of the dispensation of the law and into grace! He has made a way of escape from every temptation, trial and test and the directions to the pathway is written in the precious, powerful and pure blood of the paschal lamb!

He has placed His name on us and given us the Ring of Sonship and clothed us in the Robe of His Beloved!

Ring Giver

He placed on our finger a ring symbolizing reconciliation as the Father did with the prodigal son and declared us no longer bastards and wayward. We are positionally Sons of the most High God! He further consummates the marriage of the Bridegroom by placing a ring inside of us that says we are his beloved, sealed in our spiritual hearts. Because he consummates with Spirit and not with Flesh as he did with Mary! He carried us into the Bridal chamber by accepting our intimacy offering and we have become one with him! Through spiritual sanctification, renewal came into my life and He released me from the defilement of the impurities in my soul! He shared with me that for every person I had been intimate with, whether willingingly or unwillingly a ring was placed inside of me!

When he says that the two become one he was literally meaning that a ring is hidden inside of the uterus. It is clear to see where man is the Ring Maker in the earthly from by the shape of the circular tip of a man's penis. When he enters a womb he marks a woman internally in her secret parts as belonging to another that is not visible to the human eye! But for his good pleasure we are sealed! A covered well that cannot be defiled, a garden enclosed for private ownership! God gave me the phrase "Ring Maker" during this journey and there is a process that he has shared with me during this journey that has restored him as the rightful Ring Maker in my life at this present writing! When a husband marries his wife he places his ring, his signet, his authority inside of her and she is fitted to be his until death does them part! During this journey God confirmed this revelation to me about "The Ring Maker" while viewing a true forensics documentary, where the uterus of cadabres that had been prostitutes were studied! The scientist illustrated how the inside lining of the wall of the uterus had varying circles; he explained these were obviously marks from the varying sexual relations a woman has had over her lifetime! God is awesome and his omniscience covers all things men and women of God!! He intended us for his good pleasure on every level Spiritually to be exclusive with him and not unfaithful as Gomer was to Hosea! He has place a ring on a natural man to act as a seal of authority in the womb of his woman. Much like the wearer of a Royal Signet Ring would stamp his seal of authority in wax when sealing an envelope or document! God gave man the ring he needed to crown his wife with physically as the "Ring Giver" as he had spiritually been the "Ring Giver" and empowered man to be the physical "Ring Maker" and God to be the spiritual ring maker, as two become one in the spirit; and in the flesh!

Whose wife are you ladies? Whose husband are you gentlemen! We perish for a lack of knowledge; to have been taught like this we would have treated ourselves with much greater respect on all accounts! God Be Praised! SELAH!

Ring Maker

God is the maker of all things! He made the World, so that he could sit on the circle of the earth! He made the Galaxies and Solar Systems, and the concept of circular motion. He exist and we exist because we live and move and have our being in him. Every life bearing creation from God exist in a circle.

The stem of a flower is circular (tubular), the trees are circular and the males penis is circular, and the womans vaginal opening is circular.

This circular notion is perpetuated through the Life Cycle of Man and the Universe. God placed a ring embosser on the tip of a mans' penis that would create an imprint in the wall of a womans uterine lining that would mark her as his in the hidden parts. Selah!

Women think on this – how many men have placed a ring inside of you! Stop and think about this, could this be why so many marriages are in trouble. Because of the hauntings and clanging of rings inside that remind us of the way it use to be! Men think on this – how many women have you left your ring inside of, luring you to come back for seconds for old times sake! Your visual memory bank rolls out that footage more than you care to admit!

(Smile) God has it all under consideration children. We are suffering in our hearts; some consciously and some unconsciously because of the hidden rings that lay inside of us where we have collected inside of us as women and men have deposited! Sometimes we are given different rings by suitors and we keep them and wear them on every finger if necessary! Can you think with me for a moment that your outward display is a mirror to what is going on inside of your uterus. You keep the rings because you feel entitled to keep them and display them, and you cannot get pass the memories of the rings inside of you! Could there be a connection? Just a thought?

Ask God about it! Can you envision those rings stacked up on your fingers are stacked up inside of you while you are intimately involved with the next person.

They can't reach your heart because of the traffic jam inside, and men you can't give your heart for remembering all of the rings you gave away and who you gave them to and why you gave them away! So she can't get into your heart because there is no room to receive her gift inside of your heart! Old haunted houses!

Ring Wearer

How many rings are you still wearing my Sister, and how many ring receipts are you carrying in your pocket my Brother?

The wearer of a ring given upon betrothal, proposal or marriage is in covenant "Hased" just as God is in covenant with us! He has placed a ring of reconciliation upon our right hand and received us into the fellowship of his dear children and saints of God!

We are never to take lightly the covenant we carry in our hearts because of the fulfillment of the plan of salvation. Many of us wear multiple rings on both hands for decorative reasons. When we wear a ring on the left wedding finger it is forever a ring that we enter into with the intent to stay in covenant forever.

Think about it when that ring is placed on your finger you slide into it with tenderness and reverence and adoration for the one who is placing it on your finger.

You are so desirous of making this last forever! The ring that you receive at salvation is forever, unless you take the ring off and turn back to your old ways! Yet, God declares in Revelations that he is married to the backslider – he never never divorces us!

How many newly engaged women do you see walking around with a sad demeanor, or glum look on their faces! I have never seen one! Even when a man is engaged he has a certain look about him and a look in his eyes when he sees her walk in the room! When we receive Christ into our hearts it is him placing his imprint in our inward man, and we are so full of excitement and we want to run and tell everybody about this experience we had!

Just like the woman at the well in Samaria! I recall what the old saints would say, it gets sweeter and sweeter as the days go by! Never understood that until I came to know him fully for myself, and now I too consider it getting sweeter and sweeter as the days go by! I hope that I even look more like him! When married couples have been together for awhile they start to resemble each other, don't they? Well, we should as the ring wearer of salvation look more like the ring giver too!

We could take this much deeper, but the intent here is to steer you into the marriage supper, because the bride groom cometh! Will you be ready Don't be left out like the five foolish virgins without any oil in their lamp! It is time for you and I too manifest as the Sons and Daughters of the Most High God!

Reign

He has elevated us to a new position of righteousness and spread a robe on us and called us royalty (worthy) to be in his presence. Endued with certain rights and authority to reign and have dominion as he originally intended! Have you seen a reigning King or Queen who always stands up, reigning requires we take our rightful seats! We have been made heirs and joint-heirs through Christ Jesus! We are seated in heavenly places.

You can stand and rule, but you can not stand and reign! Reigning rulers occupy seats assigned for them for the duration and a ruler must come to rest in that office by being seated and receiving the benefits of reigning his kingdom! He daily loads us with benefits!

We are the ones who wander the wilderness like vagabonds because we are still living on Manna and not feasting at the Kings Table! The Table has been set now for awhile for us!

CHAPTER 5

Detours that Delay Destiny

5- Detours that Delay Destiny

Is this a detour or an exit I am about to take An exit is a path that has been introduced along the thoroughfare of a highway because at some point you will need to stop for gas, food, clothing and such. Once you have gotten what you needed you can return to the main thoroughfare. A detour is introduced when the primary route is under construction or an unforeseen event has occurred up ahead. Prior to arriving at the exit or detour there are markers, road signs along the path letting you know there is an alternate route approaching that will get you to the original destination if you take it.

The detour will get you back on the primary path at the end if you don't get caught up in the scenery along the path of the detour!

Sometimes life is like that, we encounter circumstances that require us to shift priorities, repair, refuel or restore ourselves at rest stops, gas stations or a mechanics garage periodically!

But once we use the detour as it was intended we should be back on the primary route headed to our original destination! Yes or No?

The problem we often face is that we allow the detour to become a permanent exit! We see someone or something that catches our attention or interest and we grant them access into our original plans. Sometimes this decision only causes a few minutes delay. Then other times they can cause days, months or years delay depending on the decision. We get cozy and comfy and try to make what should have been temporary detours along the way towards we were originally headed into permanent ones.

Remember, Satan is cunning and will not tempt us with junk along the path of righteousness, but with things we like and desire!

We see it, we like it, we entertain it, we engage the thought of possessing it and ultimately we being to succumb to the novelty of it all.

This detour now becomes an exit! Because you have made a decision not to pass through the area and get back on the main route, but to unpack and settle for what you found. Hoping for happiness, but becomes temporary happiness riddled with painful regrets.

For others we are second place prize or runner-up to the true reward is what we become willing to settle for! We settle for the fig leaf when we were promised the whole tree! I ponder in my mind was the tree of life a fig tree because the fig tree is know for its medicinal properties throughout the middle eastern region. Anyway does no really matter in the scheme of this conversation, because the point is why settle! Adam and Eve used the leaf of the fig tree to cover their nakedness and was driven from the place of reigning into hiding in the place they were meant to reign! God had already promised them the entire garden of Eden, and they settled for the fig leaf! Their seed was abandoned and their place of reign abdicated! They chose the lust of the eye, the pride of life and the lust of the flesh for one piece of fruit and had to use a leaf to cover up their impropriety!

He (God) said that he would provide seed to the Sower! Some portion of that seed is meant to be planted, harvested and not eaten! Some seed is for consumption! When a detour becomes an exit it is a decisions that you have arrived at your intended destination and are no longer interested in continuing on your original journey.

We miss the true harvest that is plenteous and settle for the poor mans lot!

This causes us to feel cheated, despair, disappointment and disallowed! Ultimately we become angry! And that becomes the downward spiral for the entry of shadows, turnings and darkness to besiege, best and belay us!

Let's look at this anger that is burning inside of us because it is bitterness' root that has delayed many of us!

Delayed and Angry

Recall that "Anger means affliction, grief, narrow, and to strangle. A strong feeling of displeasure and usually of antagonism, rage. (word study adapted from Zodhiates "The Complete Word Study Dictionary)

> Angere: (Latin) = to strangle
> Anchein: (Greek) = to strangle
> Enge: (Old Eng.) = narrow
> Angr: (Old Nor.) = grief
> Anger: (Mid. Eng) = affliction

In Summary: Anger: means emotional excitement, (induced) by intense displeasure. Anger the most general term, names the reaction; but in itself conveys nothing about the intensity or the justification or manifestation of the emotional state of one who is angry.

Synonym: according to Websters New Collegiate Dictionary means: one or more words or expressions of the same language that have the same or nearly the same meaning in some or all senses. Synonyms of anger from Zodhiates; Complete Word Study Dictionary.

Ire

Greater intensity with an evident display of feeling (color change).

Rage

Loss of self-control from violence of emotion (screaming).

Fury

Overmastering destructive rage merging on madness.

Indignation

Stresses righteous anger at what one considers unfair, mean or shameful.

Wrath

Orge (3709) - covet after, desire. Wrath, anger as a state of mind.

In Contrast

Thumos (2372) indignation, wrath as the outburst of a vengeful mind. Aristotle says that orge, is anger accompanied with grief. Mark 3:5

Implies either rage or indignation but is likely to suggest a desire or intent to revenge or punish. Anger uncontrolled and lingered in opens the door for the adversary to bring about the works of the flesh. The strong man which was once bound, is given legal permission to become unfettered and bring in seven times more guests than what were there before. While in anger, we enter into resentment, self-vindication, bitterness, grief, criticism, judgmentalism, envy and strife to name a few.

When anything besides the love and peace of God rules in your heart, you are on dangerous territory! He has made us free and we entangle ourselves again with the yoke of bondage. I have seen many disappointments and betrayals in my life, and have walked in anger and been made free, and walking free as he intended me to be.

And having become entangled again on occasion, but GOD is faithful! Speak to yourself wholeheartedly, because it is stronger of a life governed by salvation each time to break free from.

On this journey there will be opportunities to become distracted by rocks, pebbles, boulders, material possession, life's issues and personal relationships. We can get distracted and in a brief moment lose valuable time on the clock if we stay too long at the fair!

A God has time, purpose and your season under control, but we must trust him, look at him as Jesus looked at him, with belief that he is well able to perform and watch over his word!

Many of us have boat loads of prophecies and words of knowledge that have been spoken to us on paper, cassette, video tape, and in our memory banks, and we are wondering when will it come to pass!

Time and time goes by and we still hold on to what we have been told. But, when I discovered that when you are no longer self-destructively living out your destiny but aiming at completing the intended purpose of God for your life!

Thankful am I, for the time that seems lost to me because if I had manifested in my destiny sooner, I would have been like a bull in a china cabinet and self-destructed!

Thank God for the delays! Because as long as you stay on his original plan they do not become denials! When God speaks a word over your life he Is Well ABLE to perform it right then and there, but it is our frame that would be crushed if he did perform it right then and there because we were not ready to bear the weight of the blessing and would crack under its magnificence!

Wait on the Lord and be of good courage and again I say wait! Though the vision tarries wait for it for in the end it shall speak and not lie! He who has begun a good work in you in is able to perform it until the day of completion!

It is when we enter into a rest and assurance that we are the workmanship of his hand and our times are in his hand! He knows that if our eye be full of light, then our whole body is full of light. It is 'In His presence that there is fullness of joy, and treasures forever.' Have you ever noticed the countenance change on an individual when they are angry, some get red, others get darker than their true color; that is an example of shadow or turning."

There is no darkness or deception in his presence. It is like replacing a white lamp shade with a dark or black lampshade on a lit lamp!

Defiled

"Every good gift and every perfect gift is from above, and cometh down from the Father of lights, with whom is no variableness, neither shadow or turning. Of his own will begat he us with the word of truth, that we should be a kind of firstfruits of his creatures.

Wherefore my beloved brethren, let every man be swift to hear, slow to speak, slow to wrath: For the wrath of man worketh not the righteousness of God.

Wherefore lay apart all filthiness and superfluity of naughtiness, and receive with meekness the engrafted word, which is able to save your souls."

We are led astray by our own desires and lusts!

The Pride of Life

I John 2:16 says, "For all that is in the world, the lust of the flesh, and the lust of the eyes, and the pride of life, is not of the Father, but is opf the world. Verse 17 says "And the world passeth away, and the lust thereof: but he that doeth the will of God abideth for ever." Proverbs 6:16 records clearly that God hates! What does he hate "These six things the Lord hates, yes, seven are an abomination to Him:

1. A proud look, 2. a lying tongue, 3. hands that shed innocent blood, 4. a heart that devises wicked plans, 5. feet that are swift in running to evil, 6. a false witness who speaks lies, and 7. and one who sows discord among the brethren.

Oh That I May Know Him

We are seeds of promise through Abraham and sealed until the day of his coming through Jesus Christ' resurrection!

Through the resurrection that transplanted seed and beating heart is pushed through into the earth as a new creation, and thus multiplying after it's kind. Becoming a member of the family of God and the household of faith!

Reminds you of the birth of a baby, doesn't it! Unless you wanted to become stale and stunted in your development; once you are born again, you have to feed on the milk of the Word of God. And then one day you become able to stand before the world, with the heart of God being expressed toward the nations.

Remember the Bible says there will come a time when you will need to teach and not always be a student! It is now required of man to be born again from deep within the life of God to gain and maintain access to our divine inheritance.

You are now operating in the providence of God; the preservation, provision and governance of God that pertains to life and godliness.

The heart of God must be received and transplanted within us. We are not able to stand perfect and upright without his heart, a perfect heart. Less we find ourselves numbered among the things he hates and abhors!

Through the Ascension you are empowered to live the life of God and not the life of pride! We speak of the death, burial and resurrection, and barely speak of his Ascension!

As a first hand witness if it had not been for the Ascension there would not be salvation that reproduces and empowers! When he finished with the resurrection he told those who would touch him, not to – because he had not yet ascended to the Father!

He had not returned to where it all started – in the presence of God - in the heart of God!

The heart of God in Acts 11:23, in the natural realm enables us to bridge the imperfections of our flesh and enter into the place and posture of holiness. Once Christ ascended he sprinkled the blood of the spotless lamb his tithe, his sacrifice that made it established in heaven this vehicle of salvation that promises to take us into heaven! Through his ascension, he was restored and made to sit down from his work and rest and pour out his spirit on all flesh! Can't you see him seated on the right hand of the Father, interceding for us and pouring out his spirit on our raggedy, defiled flesh, commanding us to live as high as we dare! He has given each of us the vehicle of salvation in its basic form, and equipped our vehicles with varying gifts according to his good pleasure.

He gave us the keys and access to the throne room to ask in earnest for the best gifts to further accessorize our vehicle of salvation!

For the Word of God says that in Him we live, move, and have our being. He replaces our weaknesses with his strength, and thereby we become perfect in purpose. Enabled and equipped for the work of God.

Having our loins girt about with truth; the breastplate of righteousness; our feet shod with the preparation of the gospel of peace; the shield of faith; the helmet of salvation and the sword of the spirit on at all times!

We are protected and empowered to overcome and destroy the works of the enemy! Let us pull down every high thing that would exalt itself against the will of God and the advancement of His Kingdom in possession of God's Blessing!

The Commanded Blessing

- Blessed shalt thou be in the city, and blessed shalt thou be in the field.
- Blessed shall be the fruit of thy body, and the fruit of thy ground, and the fruit of thy cattle, the increase of thy kine, and the flocks of thy sheep.
- Blessed shall be thy basket and thy store.
- Blessed shalt thou be when thou comest in, and blessed shalt thou be when thou goest out.

The Lord shall cause thine enemies that rise up against thee to be smitten before thy face: they shall come out against thee one way, and flee before thee seven ways.

- The Lord shall command the blessing upon thee in thy storehouses, and in all that thou settest thine hand unto; and he shall bless thee in the land which the Lord thy God giveth thee.

- The Lord shall establish thee an holy people unto himself, as he hath sworn unto thee, if thou shalt keep the commandments of the Lord thy God, and walk in his ways

- All all people of the earth shall see that thou art called by the name of the Lord; and they shall be afraid of thee.

- And the Lord shall make thee plenteous in goods, in the fruit of thy body, and in the fruit of the cattle and in the fruit of thy ground, in the land which the Lord sware unto thy fathers to give thee.

- The Lord shall open unto thee his good treasure, the heaven to give the rain unto thy land in his season, and to bless all the work of thine hand: and thou shalt lend unto many nations, and thou shalt not borrow.

- And the Lord shall make thee the head, and not the tail; and thou shalt be above only, and thou shalt not be beneath: if that thou hearken unto the commandments of the Lord thy God, which I command thee this day, to observe and to do them:

- And thou shalt not go aside from any of the words which I command thee this day, to the right hand, or to the left, to go after other gods to serve them."

The patterned life of one who accepts, receives, and applies the divine order for his life is the righteous man who follows these steps:

"BLESSED IS the man that walketh not in the counsel of the ungodly,

nor standeth in the way of sinners,

nor sitteth in the seat of the scornful.

But his delight is in the law of the Lord; and in his law doth he meditate day and night. And he shall be like a tree planted by the rivers of water, that bringeth forth his fruit in his season;

his leaf also shall not wither;

and whatsoever he doeth shall prosper...

BUT ...

the ungodly are not so: but are like the chaff which the wind driveth away.

Therefore the ungodly shall not stand in the judgment, nor sinners in the congregation of the righteous.

For the Lord knoweth the way of the righteous; but the way of the ungodly shall perish."

A blessed man is an obedient man. That man is like a tree planted by the rivers of water. That man is not a sinner (oops) but a righteous man. One who practices the way of God and walks therein. The whole conclusion of God's purpose for our lives!

Everything else is the outworking of the in-working of Deuteronomy 28 and Psalms 1. Your calling and election are manifestations of your inward walk of righteousness, and the method by which God chooses to express your inward walk.

Such as Apostle, Prophet, Teacher, Evangelist, or Pastor.

The ability to operate with ease in these comes from the fruits of the spirit, which is the outward flow of your love walk.

The love of God is shed abroad from breast to breast! The gifts of the spirit operate like a gauge on a car measuring the amount of gas in your car. The effectiveness of your gifts are a direct relationship to the measure of anointing in your life.

Do do not get deep, and start looking around the room, and saying oh that is why sister and brother so and so is ineffective in their call. My people perish for a lack of knowledge.

The anointing is increased as we spend time in prayer, praise, worship and studying of the Word (anointing in print) of God. (II Timothy 2:15)

I know that you have read that God gave gifts unto man as he deemed. But an illustration of whether you could handle additional gifts is found in Matthew 25 in the comparison of the three(3) servants.

Matthew 25:14-30 "For the kingdom of heaven is as a man travelling into a far country, who called his own servants, and delivered unto them his goods...Let's diagram this passage!

Servant 1: And unto one he gave five talents,

Servant 2: to another two,

Servant 3: and to another one;

... to every man according to his several ability; and straightway took his journey...

Servant 2: Then he that had received two, he also gained another two.

Servant 3: But he that had received one went and digged in the earth, and hid his lord's money.

…After a long time the lord of those servants cometh, and reckoneth with them.

Servant 1: And so he that received five talents came and brought other five…His lord said unto him, well done, thou

good and faithful servant; thou hast been faithful over a few things,

…I will make you ruler over many things; enter thou into the joy of the lord.

Servant 2: He also that had received two talents came…behold I have gained two other talents.

… Well done thy good and faithful servant; thou hast been faithful over a few things,

I will make thee ruler over many things: enter thou into the joy of thy Lord.

Servant 3: Then he which had received the one talent came and said…I was afraid, and hid thy talent…lo, there thou hast that is thine.

...His lord answered and said unto him, Thou wicked and slothful servant...take therefore the talent from him, and give it unto him which hath ten talents...And cast ye the unprofitable servant into outer darkness: there shall be weeping and gnashing of teeth."

Go figure! God had allowed the lord of those servants to see the outworking of the inworking of their individual abilities. A measure of faith has been given to every man and the anointing to multiply what he has been given, and to gain even more as you are able to handle. Use what you have and you will be given more, and that is the law of multiplication according to God!

So, God's divine order is for us to be obedient and receive life. He has set before us life and death, and it is up to us to choose.

To be blessed as a result of your obedience, walk in righteousness and receive the multiplication of the commanded blessing. Which takes us right back to the beginning of what God told Adam in Genesis 1:28. "And God blessed them, (Adam & Eve) and God said unto them, these five(5) commands:

Be fruitful (show forth my glory), multiply (what I have given you), and replenish (give back to what you have received of) the earth, and subdue it (don't be afraid): and have dominion over the fish of the sea, and over the fowl of the air, and over every living thing that moveth upon the earth." Five is the number of Grace! God's Grace. His Grace is sufficient for you, his ability to work in you, through you and for you.

So you can carry out the divine order for your life:

- Be blessed fruitfully
- Be blessed to multiply
- Be blessed to replenish
- Be blessed to subdue life's Circumstances

- Be blessed to dominate over the works of Satan

"It is time to take back what the Devil has stolen from us as sons and daughters of our Heavenly Father. Come to ourselves like the Prodigal Son and be reconciled, restored and fitted for our royal garments. Even like David who rejected the use of a borrowed anointing by using Saul's' armor to fight the giant philistine Goliath. God has ours tailor made to fit us all over."

Patricia E. Adams

Six Pleasures without Gods' Delight

Now he has no problem with us having pleasure in our lives it is with what we find pleasure in that he does not appreciate from his creation. There are six (6) things he has no pleasure in us doing: Wickedness (Psalms 5:4), the legs of a man (Ps 147:10), death of the wicked (Ezek 18:23, 32:, 33:11), service of hypocrites

(Mal 1:10), Backsliders (Heb 10:38), Animal sacrifice (Heb. 10:6-8)

Bile

Tearing down anything and anybody to the point of contaminating reputations, it is a form of heresy. Where you look to discredit with a tongue full of poison.

Promiscuity

As a form of greed and excess kindred to lasciviousness! A gotta-have-it philosophy – time and place are of no consequence. You must and you will find sexual conquests and the higher you feel from each encounter, you seek to duplicate and only find that you have to increase copulation to get to the same feeling! It is never enough! This is for more than just sex, but openings of any behavior that rests in lawlessness. It is like a gateway to desires that can not find satisfaction, but must be repetitious to satisfy a ravenous appetite. I visualize an out of control person who has gone to the brink of madness without becoming mad! You push the envelope and expose yourself to great risk and peril to get satisfaction, that is never truly satisfied! He said to Balak, "Come, I shall advise you what this people 'will do to your people'" (Numbers 24:14).

They will conduct themselves in an immoral manner and become indistinguishable from Moab, lose Gods' protection and their anointing and lose their designation as the chosen of God, and then no longer to be feared!

Associations That Weaken Your Anointing

The practice of anointing with perfumed oil was common among the Hebrews. Anointing was significant in consecrating the high priest and the prophets or sacred vessels to a holy or sacred use. Rubbing oil on the leather of a shield was used to make it fit for use in war.

Also applied as an act of hospitality, burial, deliverance, medicine, gladness and as self-refreshment of the body. Weakening occurs when we are found.

Keeping Company with the Immoral

(Numbers 24:14)

Used a diabolical plot to lead the Jews astray, entice them to desert God and thus lose His support and protection. They suggested that the daughters of Moab tempt and entrap the Israelites to commit acts of immorality that would ultimately lead to acts of idolatry. Sadly, this strategy proved successful at Shittim, where the Jews succumbed to this enticement and became vulnerable to their enemies. Balaam's strategy was to divest the Jews of their unique collective character and transform them into a nation like all other nations -- no longer a people who "dwelled apart and were not to be reckoned among the nations."

Keeping Company with Those Who Launch

...Unfair Attacks

Deuteronomy 25:17-19,

Remember what Amalek did to you on your journey, after you left Egypt—how, undeterred by fear of God, he surprised you on the march, when you were famished and weary, and cut down all the stragglers in your rear. Therefore, when the Lord your God grants you safety from all your enemies around you, in the land that the Lord your God is giving you as a hereditary portion, you shall blot out the memory of Amalek from under heaven. Do not forget!

Keeping Company with Idolaters & Legalist

The Amorites adopted a new god into an already defiled religious and legal system called Marduk. They gave it the highest level of authority over all gods in the region!

They believed that there would be no life after death and lived accordingly with ruthlessness and immorality! Like the Hittites, Hivites, Perizites, Jebusites, Samaritans and Egyptians they were Idolaters and self-promoters. Not to be trusted because their motives were impure, and they never wanted to see another succeed, and at the first sign of succession it was time to come against them and cause them distress.

Keeping Company with the Lascivious

...and Barbaric

The Bible has little to say about the Hittites, and the Egyptians regarded them as barbarians. They waged war against the Egyptians that brought their empire to its knees. They were traders and moved along the coastal regions bringing the culture and world views of other peoples into any place they conquered. They were not devout, and saw place for all gods and religions to co-exist. Sort of the flavor of the day mentality! Whoever the people of the land they overthrew were worshipping they worshipped too, and this afforded the Jews to serve GOD without interference; but with grave consequences. Because of the influx of multiple religions and adoptions of various gods the society they lived in became fractured!

Keeping Company with Those Who Sow

...Discord

Genesis 13:7

There is a passage that says when you are on your way with your enemy to agree with them.

But when your enemies see infighting amongst those who are to be unified as the animosity that existed among the herdsmen of Abram and Lot.

The foreigners – the Canaanites and Perizites were living amongst them and doing what felt good to them.

When they saw the discord they took full advantage to have full reign and conduct themselves as they saw fit!

When there was no discord among the people and they walked in unity, the strength of the foreigners are weakened and they cannot rule and reign as they please!

Keeping Company with Those Involved In

...Forbidden Sex

Illicit sexual relations that uncover ones nakedness was common among the Jebsusites. "For on this day atonement shall be made for you to cleanse you of all your sins; you shall be clean before the Lord" (Leviticus 16:30). We see through this outline of the passages covering illicit sex the phrase "I the Lord am your God," "I am the Lord," and the entire parashah begins and ends with the phrase "I the Lord am your God." Then exhorting them to not do thus; "You shall not copy the practices of the Land of Egypt where you dwelt or of the land of Canaan to which I am taking you, nor shall you follow their laws." But, "My rules alone shall you observe and faithfully follow My laws." In Leviticus forbidden down to the fourth generation:

- When a man and woman are blood
- When a blood relationship with the woman's husband
- A blood relationship between the two women

The Egyptians and Canaanite people were notorious for practicing incest, lewdness and prostitution! The people of Ba'al, held a belief in a god of fertility who brings the rain. They viewed it as the seed of a man fertilizing a female! They believed the more illicit they were the more rain would come from the gods! The Israelites were tempted to walk in this same manner, and Hosea the Prophet criticized the people of his generation, "For they go off with the prostitutes and sacrifice with the harlots." (Hosea 4:13) Isaiah 58:5-8, spoke of "Those who take comfort in the gods... on a high, towering mountain did you make your bed, you also went up there to bring sacrifice" and Jeremiah 13:27 said "Your adultery and your celebration, the lewdness of your prostitution is on the hills, in the field I have seen your abominations"

During the time of plantings the behavior increased, "You loved a harlot's wages above all the harvests of grain." Because of this Abraham would not take a wife for Isaac from among the Canaanites. (Genesis 24:3-4). Abraham was told by God to perform the covenant of circumcision (Genesis 17:11) which marked his sexual organ and separated Abraham from those he dwelled among!

For this reason we are to come out from amongst those who are dissemblers, lascivious and immoral in the eyes of God.

Bad company corrupts and weakens you! God told them that when they entered the Land "You shall not let a soul remain alive. No, you must proscribe them -- the Hittites and the Amorites, the Canaanites and the Perizzites, the Hivites and the Jebusites ...lest they lead you into doing all the abhorrent things that they have done for their gods" (Deut. 20:16-18).

Israel disobeyed as found in (Judges 19:22-25). The Bible further says: "But the land which you are about to cross into and occupy, a land of hills and valleys, soaks up its water from the rains of heaven. It is a land which the Lord your God looks after, on which the Lord your God always keeps His eye from year's beginning to year's end. And it will come tpass if you carefully listen to My commandments, which I command you this day... I will grant the rain for your land in its proper time, the early rain and the late." (Deut. 11:11-14).

The Land needs rain and the belief of the Canaanite belief this dependence brings Israel to sanctification and the Chosen Land fulfills its role as the place which connects the People of Israel to God and His commandments. Therefore, when the People of Israel sin, Elijah announces a drought which lasts for three years (1st Kings 17:1; 18:1); and when the people proclaim "The Lord - He is God, the Lord - He is God", the skies grow dark with rain clouds (1 Kings 18:38-45).

Hosea said "For she did not know that it was I that gave her the corn and the wine and the oil, and multiplied unto her silver and gold, which they used for Ba'al... and I will lay waste her vines and her fig trees of which she has said, These are my hire that my lovers have given me" (Hosea 2:10-14). They creditted their acts of prostitution for the fertility of the land. Jonah said to the people of Nineveh: "In forty days time the city will be overturned" (Jonah 3:4), as punishment for their sins.

The unique relation between sexual misconduct and the Land is brought to the fore two times: "Do not defile yourselves in any of those ways, for it is by such that the nations which I am casting out before you defiled themselves. Thus was the Land defiled and I punished its iniquity and the Land spewed out its inhabitants... So let not the Land spew you out for defiling it, as it spewed out the nation that came before you" (Lev. 18:24-28)... and "Therefore keep all my statutes and all my judgments and do them, lest the Land to which I bring you to settle in spew you out" (Lev. 20:22). Why would God bring them out of Egypt if they were to continue to act like them! Why would he drive out the inhabitants of the promised land for their bad behavior, if they were going to behave as they did!

The rain that falls is attributed to God as the masculine impregnating the waters on the earth as a female who opens and receives a man. "Let the earth open and bring forth salvation" (Isaiah 46:8). These areas of sin produce behaviors that perpetuate by association.

Keeping Company with Those Who Prey On

...Others

This is an area that brings me to a point of hesitation! How much pain and how much deliverance is available to those who have been preyed upon! From this point I will say "WE" meaning I join with you right now as you are reading this text to tell you that I know what it is like to be preyed upon! Look at the next few words that you see before you with care and know that as you read the words on this page God is healing you right where you are! Those who preyed on us as children, those whom should have protected us, and those who we trusted, and those who are still alive who have harmed us! We owe ourselves a celebraton for living and not dying! We owe ourselves a debt of appreciation for pushing our way through life while we were bleeding from the wounds inside of our hearts! Hesitating in going further with you in this text because we are uncovering an area that many of us have kept hidden. Please know that in the midst of where you are and who may be misappropriately handling you right now – God is keeping your mind! This I know from experience! During these times He was Jehovah Shammah – the God who is present!

 Asking me now did I believe that when predators were preying on me and the answer is no! No one told me that it could be possible that God would allow a child to suffer and not seemingly do something to strike them down!

Until I came to know him not just as my Savior, bur as my Lord – did I understand how this God they say who is loving and caring could have possibly been present when I was being molested and seemingly did nothing!

Let me share a story with you and perhaps you will see him as he truly is! He is I AM that I AM!

Here goes, one day while driving to work on a busy highway in my time of worship! Seems like the car is my best place sometimes, as I was driving and thinking about what needed to be done when I arrived at work and what needed to be done after work. I began to thank him for where he had brought me from the day before and the dangers he had seen me through and the way that I knew he was going to continue to watch out for me! I began to hum a melody and sing in tongues, and suddenly he began to speak into my ear and tell me how much he loved me and how proud he was of me!

And this was wonderful, and then he said to me even when you hated me I still loved you! When he said that I became defensive and said No! No! I have never hated YOU! He said to me again you hated me, because you blamed me for what has been done to you in your life!

He said remember when you felt like I was not there for you and bad things were being done to you I said yes, he said to me are you in your right mind, and I said yes – and he said to me that is what I did for you when you were being mishandled! He then said to me remember I AM GOD!

Because I AM GOD – men have free wills and my choice is for them to serve me, but when they choose to follow their own desires and lust they harm themselves and others! My authority rests on the free will that men have to live and make choices!

We are what you call free agents, free to do what we feel and think! Yet, during those times we need to know that God is keeping record of what is being done to us and what we do to others! He says that what causes us to linger in the places of abuse spiritually and emotionally – long after the actual harm has been done is because we are holding onto the position of Judge over those who have harmed us!

We enter a state of perpetual grief, and it often manifest in both our body and spirit in forms of sicknesses and emotional distresses! We must abdicate judicial authority to God! Our emotions become entrenched in the past and this is where we have flashbacks (video replays) and we never seem to stop living the trauma!

We grieve over what we perceive is lost innocence and lost time and we never seem to completely gain freedom!

Excerpt from Volume I, Chapter 5

"...Luke 1:68-79 reads "Blessed be the Lord God of Israel; for he hath visited and redeemed his people. And hath raised up a horn of salvation for us in the house of his servant David:...that we should be saved from our enemies, and from the hand of all that hate us; To perform the mercy promised to our fathers, and to remember his holy covenant; The oath which he sware to our father Abraham, That he would grant unto us, that we being delivered out of the hand of our enemies might serve him, all the days of our life... to give knowledge of salvation unto his people by the remission of their sins,... To give light to them that sit in darkness and in the shadow of death, to guide our feet into the way of peace."... Hebrews 8:10-13,9:12. Jesus seals the void and restores the "Zoe," the oneness of the God life with abundant "dunamis" power.

He has brought us reconciliation, peace, access, hope/joy, perseverance, character, and love. We received a change of wills, from "I" will to "Your" will and the power supply to back it up. We are no longer victims but witnesses of the restoration. We are now salt not poison, the light not darkness, the branches not briers, the doers not just hearers, ambassadors and not anti-christ, and stewards and not squanderers. We can then rejoice, because we are reclothed, reconciled, restored, regenerated, justified, and sanctified.

So that we might have rest, receive instruction, armed for battle, prosperous, joyful, and full of praise. A born again believer is no longer separated by his self-willed, selfish desires of individualism to gratify his fleshly lust.. Our ship is no longer on a course of spiritual destruction and spiritual starvation.

But we are in possession of a vision, hearing ears, a testimony, an inheritance of one who has been given a mandated purpose, destiny and oneness in God through Christ Jesus…

II Corinthians 3:2-3 "Ye are our epistle written in our heart, known and read of all men: Forasmuch as ye are manifestly declared to be the epistle of Christ ministered by us, written not with ink, but with the Spirit of the living God; not in tables of stone, but in fleshy tables of the heart."…

Luke 15:17-24,31 "And when he came to himself,…but when he was yet a great way off, his father saw him, and had compassion, and ran, and fell on his neck, and kissed him…the foreskin that was removed from the Jewish male was symbolic of God rolling the reproach off of our lives.

When the Angel rolled the stone away from Jesus' tomb, that too was symbolic of God rolling the reproach off of man permanently. "WHAT SHALL we say then Shall we continue in sin, that grace may abound God forbid, How shall we, that are dead to sin, live any longer therein."

Seven Pleasures of Gods' Delight

Pleasure is a desire, inclination, source of delight or joy according to Romans 8:32. God wants us to have pleasure, because he made us for his good pleasure! It is the excess of anything that leads to our destruction!

"Having predestinated us unto the adoption of children by Jesus Christ to himself, according to the good pleasure of his will" Ephesians 1:5 and Revelation 4:11 "Thou art worthy, O Lord, to receive glory and honour and power: for thou hast created all things, and for thy pleasure they are and were created."

He takes pleasure in seven (7) things when his people: Prosper (Ps 35:27), do his will (Ps 103:21), men that fear him (Ps. 147:11), his own people (Ps 147:4), giving the kingdom to the little flock (Lk 12:32), Saints enjoying the fullness of God (Eph. 1:5,9) and working in men as he desires (I Thess. 1:11)

CHAPTER 6
The Last Word

6 – The Last Word

A Pediform is as the figure to the right it resembles a foot in shape. Oswald Chambers, stated "…If you select your own spot, you will prove an empty pod.  If God sows you, you will bring forth fruit. It is essential to practise the walk of the feet in the light of the vision." He is the final authority in the earth, and it looks like He has already put his foot down and has had the Last Word!

It is up to you to make your calling and election sure, and to do that we must move past the detours of speaking comfortably to the people! The Bible says that he will teach us how; "Numbers 27:17, 17 Which may go out before them, and which may go in before them, and which may lead them out, and which may bring them in; that the congregation of the LORD be not as sheep which have no shepherd " and II Chronicles 1:10-11, "10 Give me now wisdom and knowledge, that I may go out and come in before this people: for who can judge this thy people, that is so great? 11 And God said to Solomon, Because this was in thine heart, and thou hast not asked riches, wealth, or honour, nor the life of thine enemies, neither yet hast asked long life; but hast asked wisdom and knowledge for thyself, that thou mayest judge my people, over whom I have made thee king: "

Set Your Face like Flint

Jesus laid down his life for us voluntarily! This meant he had to face opposition to the promise God had made him for the redeemer of man! Before you can walk into what God has already predestined for you – you will face opposition.

Jesus' ministry is divided into stages if you would. He went through the period of "Opposition" - determined to fulfill the promise he made to his Father! Prepare me a body and I will redeem man! Here we are bodies – going through a period of preparation that proceeds the manifestation of the promises of God! Which are yes and amen! Jesus set his face toward the attack of rejection, hardship, suffering, discouragement and persevered. When we turn toward the opposition our faces contort in disdain and discomfort and dis-ease but one day we look up and our faces no longer demonstrate that we have been disquieted. Because we have endured and become strenghtend, more experienced and stable in whom we believe in!

Isaiah 50:7 "...therefore have I set my face like flint and I know I shall not be ashamed."

And in Luke 9:51 "…It is said of Him that … he steadfastly set his face to go to Jerusalem."

Flint is a rock that is formed as a result of pressure from a soft type of rock. But it has multiple thin layers that are compressed together that gives it the appearance of being solid. This rock can be used to sharpen cutlery and start fires! Jesus was unshakeable – he endured like a good solider! He set his focus on his promise and the ability of God – His Father to perform whatever he needed! In Ezekiel 3:9 God said to Ezekiel "…As an adamant harder than flint have I made thy forehead: fear them not, neither be dismayed at their looks, though they be a rebellious house." To Jeremiah in Chapter 1:18 God said "For behold, I have made thee this day a defenced city, and an iron pillar, and brasen walls against the whole land…" These passages all speak of Jesus as well!

To get to the promise you must trust God even when you can not trace Him!

Attitude will determine your altitude! Jesus did not let the opposition turn him bitter or cause him to turn back from what God had sent him to do! He said he came to work the work of the one who sent him! Don't get bitter get better!

Prelude to Promises, Prophesies & Players

The promises of God are "Yes" and "Amen." The Prophecies spoken from the mouth of "His Prophets" are based on the Word of God. God's Word is established and setted in heaven forever! The Players are recorded throughout history past and present of having changed when a player was unwilling to participate!

The playbook as you will is the same – but the players have been recorded as having been replaced, repositioned and eradicated from the game plan. It has taken years of living and seeking God to show me the manifestation of the prophecies over my life to get this revelation. One day when I told God that I did not want to hear another prophet speak another word over me, did not want to go to another Prophetic Summit or Conference or receive a word over my life by the laying on hands until I saw the manifestation of the trunk load I already had! I asked him to teach me how to walk out the prophecies that were already spoken! How to seek his face for the fulfillment of his promises over my life! The word of God that was given to me was "Teach me your ways O' Lord that I may observe them with my whole heart."

 Step-by-Step God walked me through his plan for my life as I could handle. When God shared Jeremiah 29:11 with me it literally peeled scales off of my eyes.

There was a substance that slothed off of my eyes for several days.

At first I was afraid and thought I should seek medical attention, and he spoke a word of comfort into my heart that he was peeling off religious bondage from eyes to allow me to see as He desired for me to see HIM! In the fullness of HIS glory! One can not comprehend the light in the darkness! One can not see when there is a shadow and a visual impairment. We need to have our hearts lightened and enlightened to receive the light of the Gospel of Jesus Christ!

Paul or rather Saul of Tarsus was blinded by that light on the road to Damascus! That is what happens in the life of anyone who tries to perceive the light without the right vision or eyes! It will blind you first and force you to denounce yourself and see yourself as God sees you before He restores sight to the blind! How awesome! The man laying at the Gate Beautiful had come to the end of what his state of being was in the sight of God! At that point he received his sight! We couild go into this a bit more theologically, but remember you are called to study to show yourself approved. You search it out and see what God has in store for you!

Promises

When we entered into this universe we were wrapped in at least one promise! That one being that a mans life is but a few days, and filled with much sorrow! That when a child is born into this world we should cry!

But beyond that promise are the promises that God made to Abraham, to make him a father of many nations! And beyond that he promised us that we would rule and reign with him if we would endure hardness like a good soldier!

Prophecies

Let me see a show of hands right here! How many of you as far as you can remember have prophecies that have been spoken over your life that have not come to pass Some recorded on cassette tapes, others written in spiral note books and others indelibly written on the table of your heart! We are asking God how long before they manfiest! When God – when! A trunk full of prophecies and very little manfiestation, or a whole lot of manifestation! Some travel from one prophetic conference and summit and collect them as often as possible – yet they have not seen fulfillment!

Players

This should bring peace to those who have gained a determination that will not flinch in the face of adversity.

God revealed this to me during a time that I was staggering at the promises of God!

He pointed me to the word and took me through it like Job, when Jobs wife was indicting God! Where were you Job, God said when I!

Well he said to me in the beginning was the Word! And I said to Adam be fruitful, multiply and have dominion over the earth! Well he failed to do this as God had ascribed it to him! He was replaced with Jesus! When Abraham begat Ishmael instead of waiting on God for Isaac! When Moses disobeyed God he was replaced by Joshua! Well the discourse could go on, but the point was that he told me that the Promises of God are Yes and Amen! The Prophecies of God confirm the Word of God over my life! The Players are SUBJECT to CHANGE! Let me repeat this – Promises stay the same, prophecies stay the same, but he players do what are subject to change!

  We must hold fast to that which is good! We must not get so caught up on the players that we cannot accept the promises and prophecies if the players are not who they were originally when we started out!

That ought to free somebody and manifest a lot of prophecies! What God said is his own immutable and unchangeable Word! That will never change! The prophecies that have come to you built on the promises of God are a confirmation of his promises! The players are free-will participants ad God will not cross their free will. They are entitled to play the role or not play the role in your world! Which would you rather have 2 out of the 3 not changing and the assurance that he who has begun a good work in you is able to carry it out to completion! So what – as long as he keeps his Word, why be concerned about the who, what, how, when and where! A lot of this would be resolved it we would catch the mind of God – whoever bows out of the play of your life – their replacement is greater! He will not give you less than, because God is a God of increase! When he decreases in a situation it is for the good of them who love him! He knows the story from beginning to end!

Why not trust the middle part (the details) to him! Trust him even when you can not trace HIM! It is okay when the sins of the fathers have rode you like a pony express rider under the high noon sun! God says to us you may have taken a detour but He has a way that gets us to our appointed place at the appointed time!

Detoured, Delayed but Still Destined

Psalms 40 Confidence, Obedience in God & David's prayer to be delivered from evils and iniquities!

1 I waited patiently for the LORD; and he inclined unto me, and heard my cry. 2 He brought me up also out of an horrible pit, out of the miry clay, and set my feet upon a rock, and established my goings. 3 And he hath put a new song in my mouth, even praise unto our God: many shall see it, and fear, and shall trust in the LORD. 4 Blessed is that man that maketh the LORD his trust, and respecteth not the proud,

nor such as turn aside to lies. 5 Many, O LORD my God, are thy wonderful works which thou hast done, and thy thoughts which are to us-ward: they cannot be reckoned up in order unto thee: if I would declare and speak of them, they are more than can be numbered. 6 Sacrifice and offering thou didst not desire; mine ears hast thou opened: burnt offering and sin offering hast thou not required. 7 Then said I, Lo, I come: in the volume of the book it is written of me, 8 I delight to do thy will, O my God: yea, thy law is within my heart. 9 I have preached righteousness in the great congregation: lo, I have not refrained my lips, O LORD, thou knowest. 10 I have not hid thy righteousness within my heart; I have declared thy faithfulness and thy salvation: I have not concealed thy loving-kindness and thy truth from the great congregation. 11 Withhold not thou thy tender mercies from me, O LORD: let thy loving-kindness and thy truth continually preserve me.

12 For innumerable evils have compassed me about: mine iniquities have taken hold upon me, so that I am not able to look up; they are more than the hairs of mine head: therefore my heart faileth me. 13 Be pleased, O LORD, to deliver me: O LORD, make haste to help me. 14 Let them be ashamed and confounded together that seek after my soul to destroy it; let them be driven backward and put to shame that wish me evil. 15 Let them be desolate for a reward of their shame that say unto me, Aha, aha. 16 Let all those that seek thee rejoice and be glad in thee: let such as love thy salvation say continually, The LORD be magnified.

17 But I am poor and needy; yet the Lord thinketh upon me: thou art my help and my deliverer; make no tarrying, O my God.

Jeremiah 29:11

8 For thus saith the LORD of hosts, the God of Israel; Let not your prophets and your diviners, that be in the midst of you, deceive you, neither hearken to your dreams which ye cause to be dreamed. 9 For they prophesy falsely unto you in my name: I have not sent them, saith the LORD. 10 For thus saith the LORD, That after seventy years be accomplished at Babylon I will visit you, and perform my good word toward you, in causing you to return to this place. 11 For I know the thoughts that I think toward you, saith the LORD, thoughts of peace, and not of evil, to give you an expected end. 12 Then shall ye call upon me, and ye shall go and pray unto me, and I will hearken unto you. 13 And ye shall seek me, and find me, when ye shall search for me with all your heart. 14 And I will be found of you, saith the LORD: and I will turn away your captivity, and I will gather you from all the

nations, and from all the places whither I have driven you, saith the LORD; and I will bring you again into the place whence I caused you to be carried away captive.

Gifts and Callings

Romans 11:25-32

25 For I would not, brethren, that ye should be ignorant of this mystery, lest ye should be wise in your own conceits; that blindness in part is happened to Israel, until the fulness of the Gentiles be come in. 26 And so all Israel shall be saved: as it is written, There shall come out of Sion the Deliverer, and shall turn away ungodliness from Jacob: 27 For this is my covenant unto them, when I shall take away their sins. 28 As concerning the gospel, they are enemies for your sakes: but as touching the election, they are beloved for the fathers' sakes. 29 For the gifts and calling of God are without repentance. 30 For as ye in times past have not

believed God, yet have now obtained mercy through their unbelief: 31 Even so have these also now not believed, that through your mercy they also may obtain mercy. 32 For God hath concluded them all in unbelief, that he might have mercy upon all.

The Conclusion of the Matter

Know ye not that your body is the temple of the Holy Ghost which is in you, which ye have of God, and ye are not your own" (I Corinthians 6:17, 19).

James 1:27 says "Pure religion and undefiled before God and the Father is this, to visit the fatherless and widows in their affliction, and to keep himself unspotted from the world." Psalms 119:1 says "Blessed are the undefiled in the way, who walk in the law of the Lord. Blessed are they that seek him with the whole heart."

Hebrews 7:26-27 says "For such an high priest

became us, who is holy, harmless, undefiled, separate from sinners, and made higher than the heavens; Who needeth not daily, as those high priests, to offer up sacrifice, first for his own sins, and then for the people's: for this he did once, when he offered up himself." The line has been clearly drawn between the sinner and the righteous, which side do you see yourself on In I Peter 1:3-5 it confirms the conclusion of our oneness, "Blessed be the God and Father of our Lord Jesus Christ, which according to his abundant mercy hath begotten us again unto a lively hope by the resurrection of Jesus Christ from the dead, To an inheritance incorruptible, and undefiled, and that fadeth not away, reserved in heaven for you, Who are kept by the power of God through faith unto salvation ready to be revealed in the last time." (*Bold Author's)

"As Tripartite beings we must seek as Christians and children of God to maintain an open line of communication with the Trinity. No man cometh to the Father but by me, and that he has not left us comfortless, but has sent the blessed Paraclete the Holy Spirit to lead us into all truth. It is time for the Body of Christ to get down off the cross and accept the original way of life for our Fathers' creation "man."

'He has not given us the spirit of fear "the natural man" but of power, and of love, and of a sound mind.' (II Timothy 1:7; paraphrased) All of this is ours...but though our outward man perish, yet the inward man is renewed day by day. 'For ye have not received the spirit of bondage (ADAM) again to fear, but ye have received the spirit of adoption, whereby we cry, Abba, meaning Father ... For the creature (man) was made subject to vanity, not willingly, but by reason of him (ADAM) who hath subjected the same in hope.' (Roman 8:15,20; paraphrased)

Namely, the Father, The Son and The Holy Spirit. It is their way of renewing themselves in us. The Father is the giver of all and the Son of God became the only offering, the atonement, the sacrificial and perfect lamb for the sins of the world. Thereby, closing the doors of sin and death. The Holy Spirit is the source of our new found source of life. This source is the power of God unto salvation, life abundant, divine health, and eternal life.

The object of our affection as born again believers should be the Trinity. Why Because Jesus said no man cometh to the Father but by me, and that he has not left us comfortless, but has sent the blessed Paraclete/Holy Spirit to lead us into all truth.

The Holy Spirit is the line of communication between our Father to his children, with Jesus as the Mediator between us.

The world and the church suffers from a lack of Fathers. But the worst part of this dichotomy is that the church has an exclusive Father that we neglect. The Holy Spirit is performing this scripture in the Body of Christ this hour, "Behold, I am going to send you Elijah the prophet before the coming of the great and terrible day of the LORD. And He will restore the hearts of the fathers to their children and the hearts of the children to their fathers, lest I come and smite the land with a curse" Malachi 4:4-6.

Let the Redeemed of the Lord Say So

"...Luke 1:68-79 reads "Blessed be the Lord God of Israel; for he hath visited and redeemed his people. And hath raised up a horn of salvation for us in the house of his servant David:...that we should be saved from our enemies, and from the hand of all that hate us; To perform the mercy promised to our fathers, and to remember his holy covenant; The oath which he sware to our father Abraham, That he would grant unto us, that we being delivered out of the hand of our enemies might serve him, all the days of our life… to give knowledge of salvation unto his people by the remission of their sins,… To give light to them that sit in darkness and in the shadow of death, to guide our feet into the way of peace."… Hebrews 8:10-13, 9:12. Jesus has taken and led captivity captive, and restored and sealed the void left by such sins and seals the void and restores the "Zoe," the oneness of the God life with abundant "dunamis" power. He has brought us reconciliation, peace, access, hope/joy, perseverance, character, and love. We received a change of wills, from "I" will to "Your" will and the power supply to back it up. We are no longer victims but witnesses of the restoration. We are now salt not poison, the light not darkness, the branches not briers, the doers not just hearers, ambassadors and not anti-christ, and stewards and not squanderers.

We can then rejoice, because we are reclothed, reconciled, restored, regenerated, justified, and sanctified. So that we might have rest, receive instruction, armed for battle, prosperous, joyful, and full of praise. A born again believer is no longer separated by his self-willed, selfish desires of individualism to gratify his fleshly lust.. Our ship is no longer on a course of spiritual destruction and spiritual starvation.

But we are in possession of a vision, hearing ears, a testimony, an inheritance of one who has been given a mandated purpose, destiny and oneness in God through Christ Jesus...II Corinthians 3:2-3 "Ye are our epistle written in our heart, known and read of all men:

Forasmuch as ye are manifestly declared to be the epistle of Christ ministered by us, written not with ink, but with the Spirit of the living God; not in tables of stone, but in fleshy tables of the heart."...Luke 15:17-24,31 "And when he came to himself (the prodigal son),...but when he was yet a great way off, his father saw him, and had compassion, and ran, and fell on his neck, and kissed him. This is a circumcision of heart and not of the flesh when the Father restored his son it came from the heart of a Father. The foreskin that was removed from the Jewish male was symbolic of God rolling the reproach off of our lives. When the Angel rolled the stone away from Jesus' tomb, that too was symbolic of God rolling the reproach off of man permanently…"WHAT SHALL we say then Shall we continue in sin, that grace may abound God forbid, How shall we, that are dead to sin, live any longer therein" We live in a world that is influenced by the internal environment of the womb! When a child is concieved it is shapened in iniquity! When that iniquitous child is born it comes into this world ready to enact and act out whatever has been coded into its DNA from the womb!

This is what I am referring to when I say in the meanwhile and in the between time! We are positioned between ALPHA and OMEGA, the FIRST and the LAST, the BEGINNING and the ENDING of all things to live out the life that has been given us in the world subject to the Satan, the god of this world or in the admonition of the Lord subject to the will of GOD Most High through the free pardon and plan of salvation that is available to bring us out of the penalty box and into the throne room of Grace!

While we are in between working out our soul salvation in fear and trembling we are being sanctified from being Abandoned, Aborted, Abused, Bruised, Broken, Battered, Constrained, condemned, contaminated, castrated, Degraded, Denied, Delayed, Exasperated, Exiled, Excluded, Forsaken, Forfeited, Fondled, Grabbed, Hostage, Incest, Jealousy, Killings, Lasciviousness, Mental Distresses, Neglected, Ostracized, Preyed

Upon, Quenched, Seduced, Tortured, Unwelcomed, Victimized, Whipped, XY and Z's of life. Whatever happened to you in the ABC's of life the vicissitudes of life, GOD IS still the one who knows our end from our beginning! He is our strategist, our master thinker, our giver, and righteousness, our deliverer, our one who can be touched by the feelings of our infirmities and our advocate – High Priest!

- HE has made a way of escape from all of the in between times!
- He is the first and the last, the beginning and the end, the Alpha and the Omega!

Whatever you have been through or already going through he is the way, the truth and the life (light)! Pointing out of the darkness into the marvelous light! Land ahead if you have been shipwrecked, Life preserver if you are lost at sea! Bright and Morning Star to lead you to the path of righteousness! Your Compass! Your Redeemer!

Come Away from Here and let's go up to the Mount of the Lord! Where we can cast down every high thing in your mind that has held you captive and every mountain that has hindered your progress! We are being called from the North, South, East and West – because our Father has need of US!

The whole Earth is waiting on the Manifestations of the Sons of GOD! Manifest – manifest – manifest in the name of Jesus Christ And His anointing! Amen!

Time for Newness Of Life! Simply Pray! Father in the Name of Jesus, forgive me of my sins, come into my heart and cleanse me of all unrighteousness in Jesus Name. Amen

CHAPTER 7

The Anointing of Illegitimacy

"As the mountains surround Jerusalem, so the Lord surrounds his people. If we allow God, he will bring order out of the chaos of our lives. He will surround us like the mountains of Jerusalem."

Patricia E. Adams

7- The Anointing of - Illegitimacy

The cursed anointing of illegitimacy; I speak of this as the passage that says one fly can spoil an apothecary! This can and does even exist where fathers and mothers have been physically present, but emotionally and spiritually absent. Without headship, authority or direction we are Ichabod! This is not about single-parenting but leading without a covering!

This is not an open invitation to those who are looking for justification to become parents outside of marriage, but it is a momentary discourse on submitting your present condition to God! Should you be a single parent currently, married and living as if you are a single parent because one of the parents are not engaged in parenting the child(ren)! Should you find yourself a member of a church where the parishoners are leading the church as opposed to the Pastor. Should you find yourself employed in a company where there is not a clear picture of who is at the helm! This is for you!

I pray that as we arrive at this point in our journey that we will have applied and washed ourselves in the Blood of the Lamb, and that we are ready to lift from our hearts this part of the curse as we continue on this journey of healing. Parents have abandoned, and are abandoning their children in record numbers, but the most disturbing place this is happening is in the Body of Christ. Biological parents are gone, and spiritual leaders are seen slipping and tipping. Psalms 27:10, says "When my father and my mother forsake me, then the Lord will take care of me."

I Corinthians 4:15-16, says "For though ye have ten thousand instructors in Christ, yet have ye not many fathers: for in Christ, yet have ye not many fathers: for in Christ Jesus I have begotten you through the gospel.

Wherefore I beseech you, be ye followers of me." It required a Heavenly Father concerned about his earthly children, to send the Son, and the Son to Send the Paraclete to restore the position and anointing of parenting.

Our homes, children, businesses and relationships suffer because we are ICHABOD – without a head, authority! The Father sets up the government in the home and the Mother teaches the children the laws that exist within that government. But not to despair those of you who are women without husbands training children, you have the supreme Father as your government if you will look to him in that role. And men God is the Mother for your children who will teach you how to temper and balance your government with justice!

There does not exist a finite being that can fill that role like our infinite God can!

Oppression results in an environment where there is no leadership, because women are worn down by earning wages, cooking, cleaning, negotiating, and the last thing they want to do is deal with the discipline in the home. And this is where Satan thrives! The Bible says, that if you spare the rod you hate your children! So Satan is counting on you to spare the rod. With the male Satan counts on him to overcorrect with the rod and not temper it with justice and tenderness. The Bible does not say beat, or give them what your parents gave you. Especially, if it was out of order! I know what I am speaking of, when a child is struck of out anger, or beaten until blood is drawn – you are out of order!

Never discipline a child out of anger, because anger is a fire that is fed on adrenaline, and old bad childhood memories, or abandonment of the other parent. It is not a child's fault you chose the wrong time, wrong place or an ill-prepared person to conceive with. We forget we had a choice, they didn't. This oppression shows in all forms, not having sufficiency in all areas of your life in regards to your household is oppressive.

God took Hagars baby and preserved them! What God allows is no mistake! It may happen outside of his perfect will and in his permissive will, but he will take it and weave it into the tapestry and make it work for your good!

Hagar

In the name of Jesus Christ, receive your healing now, allow God to send ministering angels to you right where you are. Touch and heal my brothers and sisters Abba, Daddy, Momma right now in the name of Jesus! Holy Ghost move upon them now as the read this prayer from the soles of their feet to the crown of their heads, touch right now in the name of Jesus, be loosed from the grave clothes, shake off the dust of decay and open your mouth and confess that right now I am free from the curse of the law of sin and death, I have been redeemed by the Blood of the Lamb, Jesus Christ and his anointing, I am set free, delivered and made whole in every area of my life. I refuse to sit in the dark and damp cave of despair and dejection, I am accepted in the beloved, I am not forsaken because you Lord have taken up my cause, I am washed clean! Right now God I choose to step into the light of the "Sun (Son)" of your delight and thank you for the chains and the cords of silver (bondage) being released from me now. I am no longer a headless man or woman "Ichabod" a rebel without any constraints from the path of evil. Constrain me father and I shall be constrained from evil, mold me in your image and I shall come forth as pure gold, refine me in the refiners fire until you can see your reflection in me.

Create in me a clean heart o' God and renew within me a right spirit, purge me with hyssop and I shall be whiter than snow, order my steps in your word, and every thought and vain imagination of my life, bring it under your control, I submit myself under your mighty hand, so that I may be able to resist the Devil and he will flee from me, not one way, but seven ways. Teach me your way and I will observe them with my whole heart. I release my mother and my father from any act of retribution or revenge, I put them in your hands to vindicate because you said that vengeance is yours, and I ask for mercy on their behalf that you would send laborers in their path to minister the glorious gospel of salvation to them. Teach me how to set boundaries in my life, in the area of all my relationships, protect and shield my heart as I learn to walk in your pure love for all of us. I will hate the sin of my forefathers and not them individually. I choose to by faith not by my feelings to forgive any act of lawlessness that my family has done to me, I ask that you would remove this from my heart as I am able to bear. Make me a living epistle before all men, let me reach back and strengthen my brethren when I have been converted, and to teach transgressors your way. Make me a blessing so that I may freely bless others with the joy of your salvation. I thank you that as I have prayed this prayer as an act of faith, trust and confidence in you and not of my feelings that I am no longer without parents, you are my parents in every area of my life from this day forward in Jesus Name I pray, Amen!

As you continue your journey day by day, second by second, minute by minute, mili-second by mili-second; keep a heart that is quick to repent and repray this prayer or any prayer that God impresses on your heart until you are standing on your own two feet.

Meanwhile everyday enter into it with a spirit and a mind of thanksgiving, thank him that all the things that you prayed today have been accomplished in your life.

Here is this prayer again converted to thanksgiving:

In the name of Jesus Christ, I thank you that I have received healing and allowed God to send ministering angels to me right where I am. I have been touched and healed by you, my Abba, Daddy, Momma. That now the name of Jesus and the Holy Ghost have moved upon me from the soles of my feet to the crown of my head. That I am loosed from the grave clothes, shaken off the dust of decay as I opened my mouth and confessed that I am free from the curse of the law of sin and death, I have been redeemed by the Blood of the Lamb, Jesus Christ and his anointing, I am set free, delivered and made whole in every area of my life.

Because, I refused to sit in the dark and damp cave of despair and dejection, I am accepted in the beloved, I am not forsaken because you Lord have taken up my cause, I am washed clean! I chose to step into the light of the "Sun (Son)" of your delight and the chains and the cords of silver (bondage) are released from me now. I am no longer a headless man or woman "Ichabod" a rebel without any constraints from the path of evil. I am constrained from evil, being molded in your image and I am coming forth as pure gold, refined in the refiners fire until you can see your reflection in me. Created in me each day a clean heart o' God and a renewed right spirit, purged with hyssop, and being made whiter than snow, you order my steps in your word, and every thought and vain imagination of my life, is under your control, I submitted myself under your mighty hand, and I am able to resist the Devil and he flees from me, not one way, but seven ways.

I am being taught your way and I will observe them with my whole heart. I released my mother and my father from any act of retribution or revenge, I placed them in your hands to vindicate because you said that vengeance is yours, and I asked for mercy on their behalf that you would send laborers in their path to minister the glorious gospel of salvation to them. You are teaching me how to set boundaries in my life, in the area of all my relationships, protecting and shielding my heart as I learn to walk in your pure love for all of us. I hate the sin of my forefathers and not them individually. I chose faith not my feelings to forgive any act of lawlessness that my family has done to me, I asked that you would remove this from my heart as I am able to bear. Make me a living epistle before all men, let me reach back and strenghten my brethren when I have been converted, and to teach transgressors your way. I am a blessing so that I may freely bless others with the joy of your salvation. I thank you that as I have prayed this prayer as an act of faith, trust and confidence in you and not of my feelings that I am no longer without parents, you are my parents in every area of my life from this day forward in Jesus Name I pray, Amen!

Ask God to reveal hurts and resentments from your experience with the absent parent. Forgive those persons; biological, adoptive or spiritual leaders. Pray for rhema – revelation of the word of God that will cause you to see this role through God's eyes.

Receive God as your father and mother and accept that his love is from everlasting to everlasting.

Let's examione another example of the curse of illegitimacy within a legitimate marriage ordained of God between Hosea and Gomer

Gomer

Hosea 2; begins with the idolatry of the people and God vowing to punish their sins and pronounces judgment on them and yet in his heart has a plan of redemption for them after they have endured the judgment he sends. This is like a parent punishing a child. Most parents ask the child do you know why I am punishing you, then tells them their punishment while telling them how much it hurts them to punish them, and the child is wondering how could that be true! Yet, in the heart of the parent they complete the punishment thinking of ways the whole time of how they can to restore the childs faith in them as a loving parent! My how this must have hurt God to see that after more or less 650 years since the exodus from Egypt the children of Israel have gone astray and whoring after other gods. They had prospered greatly in their new land and began to take the credit of their success, neglecting to give God the praise!

They began submitting sermon requests to be tailored to their own liking, and they never realized that God had gotten tired of the affront! Here God is saying to Hosea his prophet for the time to tell the children of Israel; "2:1 Say ye unto your brethren, Ammi; and to your sisters, Ruhamah. 2 Plead with your mother, plead: for she is not my wife, neither am I her husband: let her therefore put away her whoredoms out of her sight, and her adulteries from between her breasts; ..."

Whoredoms from between her breast she had given her fidelity to another, and allowed the hearts of illegitmate lovers take counsel in her soul. No longer could the scripture of Proverbs be true, that the heart of her husband safely trust in her! This wife had too many divided interests to be trusted by her husband and maker God being symbolized by Hosea.

Then God says tell them Hosea because of this that, "2:3 Lest I strip her naked, and set her as in the day that she was born, and make her as a wilderness, and set her like a dry land, and slay her with thirst. 4 And I will not have mercy upon her children; for they be the children of whoredoms. 5 For their mother hath played the harlot: she that conceived them hath done shamefully: for she said, I will go after my lovers, that give me my bread and my water, my wool and my flax, mine oil and my drink...."

All the time Gomer did not know while she was entertaining her lovers and being pimped by her lovers, that Hosea was coming to the door of her lovers and leaving provisions with them to make sure she did not want for anything! Yet, Gomer says "I will go after my lovers, that give me my bread and my water, my wool and my flax, mine oil and my drink."

How amazing it is when we take what God has done for us and attribute it to our own strength and to the strength of mere men! God has yet to do to us what was done to Israel, when God judged them his judgments were swift and severe!

He proclaims to Hosea, in "2:6 Therefore, behold, I will hedge up thy way with thorns, and make a wall, that she shall not find her paths. 7 And she shall follow after her lovers, but she shall not overtake them; and she shall seek them, but shall not find them: then shall she say, I will go and return to my first husband; for then was it better with me than now.

God would confuse her ways by making her straight places the ways she knew how to get to her lovers before, crooked and undiscernable by her until she would tire of searching for them and return back to God; symbolized by Hosea.

But before he unleashed the judgments, God reflects on how good he has been to his wife "Israel" with Hosea! Can you imagine a husband telling his friend about how good he has been to his wife and yet she continues to take him for granted, not asking for a divorce, but keeping the marriage as a mere convenience without the commitment!

God said to Hosea, "2:8 For she did not know that I gave her corn, and wine, and oil, and multiplied her silver and gold, which they prepared for Baal. 9 Therefore will I return, and take away my corn in the time thereof, and my wine in the season thereof, and will recover my wool and my flax given to cover her nakedness..." Gomer thinks that she is free to continue to live a life of whoredoms because God (Hosea) has winked at her infidelities for so long, through so many different ways and surely he has not intention of leaving her.

Because if he were he would have left before now! But God says not so, not so! I will strip her to nothing and expose her before her lovers and allow her lovers to despise her! While she would adorn herself to please her lovers and not her husband and party and revel in the splendor of all the wealth of the land afforded to her and neglect her husband!

"2:10 And now will I discover her lewdness in the sight of her lovers, and none shall deliver her out of mine hand. 11 I will also cause all her mirth to cease, her feast days, her new moons, and her sabbaths, and all her solemn feasts. 12 And I will destroy her vines and her fig trees, whereof she hath said, These are my rewards that my lovers have given me: and I will make them a forest, and the beasts of the field shall eat them. 13 And I will visit upon her the days of Baalim, wherein she burned incense to them, and she decked herself with her earrings and her jewels, and she went after her lovers, and forgat me, saith the LORD.

After all of his anger, you see it tempered with a plan of salvation, of redemption and restoration to his rightful place. But until that time there would be great constrictions upon her, the land, the creatures and their physical strength!

Hosea 2:14 Therefore, behold, I will allure her, and bring her into the wilderness, and speak comfortably unto her. 15 And I will give her her vineyards from thence, and the valley of Achor for a door of hope: and she shall sing there, as in the days of her youth, and as in the day when she came up out of the land of Egypt. 16 And it shall be at that day, saith the LORD, that thou shalt call me Ishi; and shalt call me no more Baali.

He took the valley of Achor a place known to be a place of distress and showed how he would rename the place for her sake a door of hope, and how he would turn her sorrow back into joy as when they left the slavery of Egypt. During the judgment God would be known to Israel as Baalim, meaning master and after the judgment they would return to calling him their husband "Ishi".

"2:17 For I will take away the names of Baalim out of her mouth, and they shall no more be remembered by their name." As God is a covenant maker and keeper the whole earth stands in earnest expectation for the sons of God to manifest in this present hour! Yet Hosea is told by God how this would come to pass, it speaks of a future time when war will cease and the creatures will be at peace and dwell in safety. We have proof that he is a covenant keeper whenever we see a rainbow in the sky! And this promise shall be no different that he speaks to Hosea about in Chapter 2:18 "And in that day will I make a covenant for them with the beasts of the field, and with the fowls of heaven, and with the creeping things of the ground: and I will break the bow and the sword and the battle out of the earth, and will make them to lie down safely." This time we will be his Bride for all eternity, and how we get there is through the transformation from harlotry and idolatry and penalty into a place of position of Brides whose robes have been washed in the blood of the lamb when he speaks of restoration of the relationship in 2:16 you see him expressing to Hosea what that relationship would be like in In Hosea 2:19 And I will betroth thee unto me for ever; yea, I will betroth thee unto me in righteousness, and in judgment, and in lovingkindness, and in mercies. 20 I will even betroth thee unto me in faithfulness: and thou shalt know the LORD. 21 And it shall come to pass in that day, I will hear, saith the LORD, I will hear the heavens, and they shall hear the earth; 22 And the earth shall hear the corn, and the wine, and the oil; and they shall hear Jezreel. 23 And I will sow her unto me in the earth; and I will have mercy upon her that had not obtained mercy; and I will say to them which were not my people, Thou art my people; and they shall say, Thou art my God." Hosea 2:1-23 (KJV) The anointing of illigetimacy and its power has had its back broken by the Word of His Power, the Name given above every name and the cleansing power of the Blood of the Lamb! We are the Bride whom the Bridegroom shall come for at the Wedding Feast! There is a way out of the valley of achor "trouble" and through the door of achor "hope" and it is ours today! Doesn't matter what you did or who you did it with or how far you think you may have strayed from the path; God says come home!

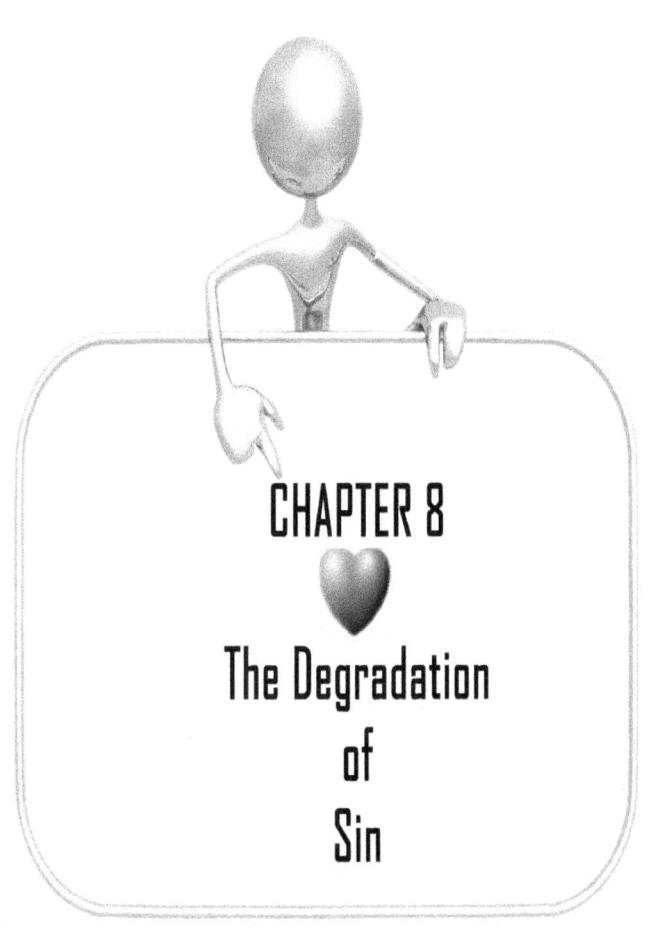

CHAPTER 8

The Degradation of Sin

8 – The Degradation of Sin

Sin is disobedience, rebellion, unbelief, ignorance, tgeh breach of a right relationship with God and his Word! It results in the disintegration of self and the disregard of the welfare of others we enteract with! It is willful and unwillfully creating a false way of living in opposition to the will of GOD! Romans 12:1-2 says that "I BESEECH you therefore, brethren, by the mercies of God, that ye present your bodies a living sacrifice, holy, acceptable unto God, which is your reasonable service. And be not conformed to this world: but be ye transformed by the renewing of your mind, that ye may prove what is that good, and acceptable, and perfect, will of God! I chose to use a discourse around some characters of the Old Testament regarding sin, because this passage I quoted above has done away with the penalty of the Old Testament. This is working backwards to bring about an appreciation for the gift of Salvation!

The Old Testament was full of those who could not walk blameless before him, because they were not endued individually with power as New Testament believers are today! Thus they labored under the effects of the fall, walking in a legalistic relationship with God and their neighbors, with themselves and the world! Strife among men and the earth! All are a result of the conception of lust, which gave birth to sin and sin gave birth to death! There were those who made it to the Hall of Faith, who were imputed as righteous because they walked worthy before God! The discourse below is about those who did not make it into the Hall of Faith, because they were overtaken with the sins of their fathers, and their fathers!

Dathan has always interested me and so I chose him to take the lead in this! It reminds me of infighting in families, which still goes on today! So maybe you too will relate! When we come to the end of ourselves I hope we come to Jesus! Each of the individuals snared by degradation have this in common and that is the loss of mental clarity! When we lift ourselves above God as gods we become delusional in our minds!

Dathan (meaning Strong)

He and his brother Abiram along with others amongst the children of Israel, decided to follow Korah whose name meant baldness, also a Levite disputes Moses and Aarons being separated from among the Levites as the only ones who were Holy enough to have the authority to lead them to the Promised Land!

Since they too were descendants of the Levites! Korah and the others perished by fire before the tent of meeting, because they offered up the incense and waived the censers containing what was symbolic fire of God.

Dathan and his brother Abiram and their families and all they owned were swallowed up in the earth while at their own tents, they refused to offer up incense and wave the censer, but nevertheless questioned Gods will in the matter of who was anointed and appointed as their leaders with their mouth, so the earth opened its mouth and swallowed them!

Then 14,700 other Israelites were stricken by plague because they spoke against Moses for the deaths of Dathan, Abiram, Korah and their group!

What is it I am trying to say to you is that the degradation of sin is not suddenly revealed, it is conceived first as lust and lust gives birth to sin! Sin gives birth to death!

James 1:13-15 says this, "Let no man say when he is tempted, I am tempted of God: for God cannot be tempted with evil, neither tempteth he any man: But every man is tempted, when he is drawn away of his own lust, and enticed. Then when lust hath conceived, it bringeth forth sin, when it is finished, bringeth forth death."

Dathan you recall if you have every watched the rendition of the Ten Commandments, never liked Moses, and it is amazing that he (Dathan) being an Israelite did not recognize Moses even as he lived in Pharoahs palace as an Egyptian!

He wanted power and he coveted and had an insatiable appetite for more than he could afford! His own lust concieved and created an environment in his soul for his ultimate demise in the wilderness!

He came from the tribe of Levi and yet he never found peace in his own estate!

I mention the names of those around, his genealogy and the meaning of the names, and to know that he could be traced back to Jacob and Leah – whose name meant "wild cow", the girl that Jacob did not love, but who would do whatever to get his attention, passed on a weakness, a generational curse to her own child Reuben her fist born son, which would later manifest itself in the soul of his descendant Dathan, whose name meant strong!

When they were headed to the promised land and they faced Pharoah (slavery) behind them and the Red Sea (faith) before them they splintered into four camps; three of doubt and one of faith and a final decree! In Exodus 14:10:14

Camps of Opinion

10 And when Pharaoh drew nigh, the children of Israel lifted up their eyes, and, behold, the Egyptians marched after them; and they were

sore afraid: and the children of Israel cried out unto the LORD.

Camp 1: Doubt

11 And they said unto Moses, Because there were no graves in Egypt, hast thou taken us away to die in the wilderness? wherefore hast thou dealt thus with us, to carry us forth out of Egypt?

Camp 2: Doubt

12 Is not this the word that we did tell thee in Egypt, saying, Let us alone, that we may serve the Egyptians?

Camp 3: Doubt

For it had been better for us to serve the Egyptians, than that we should die in the wilderness.

Camp 4: Faith

13 And Moses said unto the people, Fear ye not, stand still, and see the salvation of the LORD, which he will shew to you to day: for the Egyptians whom ye have seen to day, ye shall see them again no more for ever.

Authority of Faith

The DECREE:

14 The LORD shall fight for you, and ye shall hold your peace.

With the water before them and Pharoah behind them the faith camp stepped out and God stepped up! The Jewish tradition tells the story that they walked into the water before it split and they were neck deep in the water and it looked like they were about to drown! And that is when God parted the waters for them and they crossed over! Personally, I like this, I like this – because it sounds so like God! Do all you can do and when you have done all you can to to stand, stand still and see the salvation of the Lord! Faith is an action, and it lends itself to this tradition of thought! Simply standing at the water took no faith, because Pharoah would have destroyed them, they were commanded to "go" into the promised land and possess the land.

Which indicates forward motion on their part to get there, this camp did not stagger at the promise of God and their faith was responded to and all passed over to the other side safely! But the Egyptians were destroyed that day that pursued after God's chosen ones! There is so much more to this passage of scripture than meets the eye, the cause and effect of a spoken word and a people who had to believe before they could get the manifestation of the Word! When our level of faith meets the level of God's Word we have spiritual ignition in the atmosphere and a response is promised!

Without the abiding presence of God and the respect for the authority of God we are destined to repeat Dathan's folly and Adam and Eves!

God had placed righteous men to rule over them! Yet Dathan, whose name meant strong, did a weak thing and died a weak death!

God himself had witnessed Leah's misery as unloved of Jacob's wives, and gives her a son whose name meant he has seen my misery; and that out of this birth she would assuredly gain the love of her husband Jacob!

Reubens mother Leah for the sake of following this train of thought we will say, "Wild Cow" gives birth to a son who the Historian Josephus translates as Ra'abil, meaning wolves, but others translate it as "Behold a Son – the Lord has seen my affliction."

This same Reuben is noted as having had sex with his fathers maid which is considered incest according to jewish custom, because his father had had sex with her and she had given birth to two of his half-brothers; Dan and Naphtali! Reuben who is descended from Leah; the unloved wild cow loses his birthright to (as firstborn) to Joseph, because Jacob was angry with Reuben!

Which transfers not just the birth right, but the rights of the tribe of Reuben to become rulers over the tribes, which was then transferred to Judah! And the priesthood to rule in the house of God to Levi! While other historians argue that Reuben did not sleep with Bilhah, but did not appreciate Jacob favoring Bilhah after the death of his mother Rachel, the loved one!

Yet, Jacob the father of Judah her husbands father, Jacob the one whose name meant trickster was tricked by Tamar, the actual daughter-in-law of his son, Judah; who had been married to two of Jacobs grandsons! The first died because of his wild behavior, and the latter because he failed to sleep with his brothers wife to preserve his legacy, thus failed to obey God! Their father Judah, one of Jacobs sons would not grant permission for her to marry his last son in marriage as the custom dictated. This history attributes to Tamar playing the part of a prostitute on the highway and tricking Jacob her father-in-law into having sex with her, and concieves twins "Perez and Zerah" which by jewish law become the sons of Judah and not of Jacob! Wow!

Perez name meant bursting forth or breach, and Zerah meant shining forth because he stuck his hand out first at birth and withdrew it, so Perez became the first born!

Tamar preserves her husbands legacy through trickery, because she is desperate and yet she is found in the genealogy of Jesus!

Back to Reuben, while he was fasting and repenting for his sins, his father is on the highway being tricked by a prostitute, who is really his daughter-in-law! When Reuben, discovers what his father had done, he confesses to what he did with Bilhah the concubine and mercy was granted to him.

Because of this historians say that the Prophet Hosea was descended from Rueben as a sign of that mercy for Reubens repentance! Later Rueben again is honorable by not allowing the brothers to kill Joseph, tries to rescue him and reminds the brothers when they are accused of robbery in Egypt that it is divine punishment for what they did to Joseph! Out of this messiness descends Dathan and Abiram

Dathan's name meant strong remember and his brother Abirams' name meant my Father is an Exalted One, and their father was a Reubenite named Eliab, meaning God is Father. And Eliabs Father was Pallu a second son of Reuben, whose name meant Be Conspicuous, Extraordinary, and Pallu's father was Reuben whose name meant – Behold a Son – the Lord has seen my affliction, born of Jacob and Leah. According to the Old Testament, the sins of the fathers were visited upon their children, and the childrens teeth were set on edge!

Thank God for the grace of God through his son Jesus, who has redeemed us from this crazy curse and reminds us that no longer will the childrens teeth be set on edge or the sins of our fathers be visited upon us! Then we must not degrade ourselves any longer by symbolically re-enacting the work of salvation as the Bible says when we continue in sin! Let's examine others!

Nebuchadnezzar

His name meant (may Nabu protect my boundary stone) King of Babylon and conqueror the Davidic Jerusalem, son of Nabopolassar, meaning usurper of the throne! He placed heavy taxes on the people, and worshipped idols. He attempted to force Daniel to bow down to his Gods! Opportunity was given to him to recognize the Kingdom of God, yet he refused and his dream was fulfilled, he was driven insane and crawled around on all fours like an animal!

Daniel 4:33-34, says "The same hour was the thing fulfilled upon Nebuchadnezzar: and he was driven from men, and did eat grass as oxen, and his body was wet with the dew of heaven, till his hairs were grown like eagles' feathers, and his nails like birds' claws. And at the end of the days I Nebuchadnezzar lifted up mine eyes unto heaven, and mine understanding returned unto me, and I blessed the most High, and I praised and honoured him that liveth for ever, whose dominion is an everlasting dominion, and his kingdom is from generation to generation:"

Prodigal Son

The Father/Son Model expressing God's relationship in Luke 15:12-24 "And the younger of them said to his father, Father, give me the portion of goods that falleth to me. And he divided unto them his living! And not many days after the younger son gathered all together, and took his journey into a far country, and there wasted his substance with riotous living...and he began to be in want...and when he came to himself, he said, How many hired servants of my father's have bread enough and to spare, and I perish with hunger! I will arise and go to my father, and will say unto him Father, I have sinned against heaven, and before thee,...But the father said to his servants...for this my son was dead, and is alive again..." Alive in Christ

We are in the Year of Jubilee because the Day of Atonement has been fulfilled!

We have gained personal liberty, restoration of property and increase in wealth! The law has been fulfilled and a more excellent way has been established!

Philemon 16: says that the masters and servants are brothers, and our status is no longer slaves! We are truly liberated and allowed to participate in free enterprise and land ownership, all that has been displaced through our sinful birthrights and real property has been redeemed from corruption and injustice! Old things are passed away and behold all things have become new!

In the name of Jesus Christ, receive your healing now, allow God to send ministering angels to you right where you are. Touch and heal my brothers and sisters Abba, Daddy, Momma right now in the name of Jesus! Holy Ghost move upon them now as the read this prayer from the soles of their feet to the crown of their heads, touch right now in the name of Jesus, be loosed from the grave clothes, shake off the dust of decay and open your mouth and confess that right now I am free from the curse of the law of sin and death, I have been redeemed by the Blood of the Lamb, Jesus Christ and his anointing, I am set free, delivered and made whole in every area of my life. I refuse to sit in the dark and damp cave of despair and dejection, I am accepted in the beloved, I am not forsaken because you Lord have taken up my cause, I am washed clean! Right now God I choose to step into the light of the "Sun (Son)" of your delight and thank you for the chains and the cords of silver (bondage) being released from me now. I am no longer a headless man or woman "Ichabod" a rebel without any constraints from the path of evil. Constrain me father and I shall be constrained from evil, mold me in your image and I shall come forth as pure gold, refine me in the refiners fire until you can see your reflection in me.

Create in me a clean heart o' God and renew within me a right spirit, purge me with hyssop and I shall be whiter than snow, order my steps in your word, and every thought and vain imagination of my life, bring it under your control, I submit myself under your mighty hand, so that I may be able to resist the Devil and he will flee from me, not one way, but seven ways. Teach me your way and I will observe them with my whole heart. I release my mother and my father from any act of retribution or revenge, I put them in your hands to vindicate because you said that vengeance is yours, and I ask for mercy on their behalf that you would send laborers in their path to minister the glorious gospel of salvation to them. Teach me how to set boundaries in my life, in the area of all my relationships, protect and shield my heart as I learn to walk in your pure love for all of us. I will hate the sin of my forefathers and not them individually. I choose to by faith not by my feelings to forgive any act of lawlessness that my family has done to me, I ask that you would remove this from my heart as I am able to bear. Make me a living epistle before all men, let me reach back and strenghten my brethren when I have been converted, and to teach transgressors your way. Make me a blessing so that I may freely bless others with the joy of your salvation. I thank you that as I have prayed this prayer as an act of faith, trust and confidence in you and not of my feelings that I am no longer without parents, you are my parents in every area of my life from this day forward in Jesus Name I pray, Amen!

As you continue your journey day by day, second by second, minute by minute, mili-second by mili-second; keep a heart that is quick to repent and repray this prayer or any prayer that God impreses on your heart until you are standing on your own two feet.

Meanwhile everyday enter into it with a spirit and a mind of thanksgiving, thank him that all the things that you prayed today have been accomplished in your life.

Here is this prayer again converted to thanksgiving:

In the name of Jesus Christ, I thank you that I have received healing and allowed God to send ministering angels to me right where I am. I have been touched and healed by you, my Abba, Daddy, Momma. That now the name of Jesus and the Holy Ghost have moved upon me from the soles of my feet to the crown of my head. That I am loosed from the grave clothes, shaken off the dust of decay as I opened my mouth and confessed that I am free from the curse of the law of sin and death, I have been redeemed by the Blood of the Lamb, Jesus Christ and his anointing, I am set free, delivered and made whole in every area of my life. Because, I refused to sit in the dark and damp cave of despair and dejection, I am accepted in the beloved, I am not forsaken because you Lord have taken up my cause, I am washed clean! I chose to step into the light of the "Sun (Son)" of your delight and the chains and the cords of silver (bondage) are released from me now. I am no longer a headless man or woman "Ichabod" a rebel without any constraints from the path of evil. I am constrained from evil, being molded in your image and I am coming forth as pure gold, refined in the refiners fire until you can see your reflection in me. Created in me each day a clean heart o' God and a renewed right spirit, purged with hyssop, and being made whiter than snow, you order my steps in your word, and every thought and vain imagination of my life, is under your control, I submitted myself under your mighty hand, and I am able to resist the Devil and he flees from me, not one way, but seven ways. Iam being taught your way and I will observe them with my whole heart. I released my mother and my father from any act of retribution or revenge, I placed them in your hands to vindicate because you said that vengeance is yours, and I asked for mercy on their behalf that you would send laborers in their path to minister the glorious gospel of salvation to them. You are teaching me how to set boundaries in my life, in the area of all my relationships, protecting and shielding my heart as I learn to walk in your pure love for all of us. I hate the sin of my forefathers and not them individually. I chose faith not my feelings to forgive any act of lawlessness that my family has done to me, I asked that you would remove this from my heart as I am able to bear. Make me a living epistle before all men, let me reach back and strenghten my brethren when I have been converted, and to teach transgressors your way. I am a blessing so that I may freely bless others with the joy of your salvation. I thank you that as I have prayed this prayer as an act of faith, trust and confidence in you and not of my feelings that I am no longer without parents, you are my parents in every area of my life from this day forward in Jesus Name I pray, Amen!

Ask God to reveal hurts and resentments from your experience with the absent parent. Forgive those persons; biological, adoptive or spiritual leaders. Pray for rhema – revelation of the word of God that will cause you to see this role through God's eyes. Receive God as your father and mother and accept that his love is from everlasting to everlasting.

Also, remember whats' in a name we discussed in the previous volume how amongst the ancients a name summed up a man's history and represented his personality! Both his past was reflected in his present because they were identical, according to Herbert Locker in All the Men of the Bible, p. 366.

When a child is named it should speak of his character, that you believe the child actually possess or that which you are invoking into his life. Every time you call that name you should be drawing out of that child their destiny and one day they will rise to the occasion if nurtured in the admonishen of the Lord!

If every vulgar adjective hs been called to you or your children other than the name you gave them can you see how your future was shaped by those words! Do you see yourself doing things that were spoken to you or about you negatively? Do you see that same pattern in your children? Don't despair – God took that into consideration too, when Jesus was given his name – he was given a name that was above every name that every knee and tongue would have to bow to! Tell those things they have no authority over you if you are born again, if not receive Jesus now as our Savior and Lord! Ask him to come into your heart and save you – just like that and he will come in and dwell with you according to your hearts desire!

A good name chosen can be earned through behaving in a manner that is pleasing to God. Keeping our word, making good on promises, being on time, and being a confidante and a friend, and things like this will earn you a good name if you have been affected by negativity being spoken over you!

Even if your parents named you "Ahira" meaning brother of evil, God can take any circumstance and reverse it when you walk upright before him. After all a mans' name will be given to his wife, children and grandchildren for generations to come. Whether male or female descendants they will always carry your name!

CHAPTER 9

The Christian Who Knows the Tools in Their Toolbox

9 - The Christian Who Knows the Tools

...in Their Toolbox

The Pentateuch Relationship

The word Pentateuch is from the Greek root – penta, meaning "five" and teuchos, meaning "a tool". It refers to the first five books of the Bible known as Genesis, Exodus, Leviticus, Numbers, and Deuteronomy. They are known as "the Law".

A - Genesis (In the Beginning)

The darkness of a world without the presence of God begins the plan of redemption through Abraham! This speaks of the preservation and restorative plan of God for his people!

B – Exodus (These are the names)

Recounts the history and birth of a people who will reflect his image and show forth his character! To be His people and He their God!

Building of a place for communion with God with His People! The means for communication as a result of their communion!

C- Leviticus (He the Lord Called Unto Moses)

Set forth a law that will instruct His people on how to live before him and to humanity! Showing forth the love to God, to themselves, to others!

D- Numbers (In the Wilderness)

Consequences of disobedience are meted out because they failed to enter into their inheritance because of a lack of faith!

A remnant who believes on him will be prepared and ready to claim the inheritance that what was rightfully theirs!

E – Deuteronomy (These are the Words)

It is through obedience that the children of Israel will possess the land! They obey and receive all that God promised. Thus we exists for the Glory of God to be reflected before men in the earth and the fulfillment of salvation being preached to every creature!

Let the Redeemed of the Lord Say So!

The Christian who knows their way around their toolbox - acknowledges that God is their preserver, their holy habitation, their righteousness, their redeemer and exceeding great reward!

In Job 38: 22-23, God asked Job "Hast thou entered into the treasures of the snow? Or hast thou seen the treasures of the hail, 23Which I have reserved against the time of trouble, against the day of battle and war?"

The snow is a tool in God's toolbox and we should know why he uses the tools he uses to be skillful in His Word! The treasure of the snow hides beneath it the sprouts pushing through the earth in preparation for spring and harvest time! The treasures of the snow lying beneath it are for an appointed time. Jewish studies states the numerical value of the word snow is 333. The number 3 alone is for the trinity and the Father, and when in multiples like 333 it reflects the divinity of the Trinity. When snow touches the earth it blankets the ground and then waters the earth when it melts. Underneath the blanket it provides a covering for the rebirth and birthing of the land! Isaiah 55:9-11 states, "For my thoughts are not your thoughts, neither are your ways my ways, saith the LORD. For as the heavens are higher than the earth, so are my ways higher than your ways, and my thoughts than your thoughts. For as the rain cometh down, and the snow from heaven, and returneth not thither, but watereth the earth, and maketh it bring forth and bud, that it may give seed to the sower, and bread to the eater: So shall my word be that goeth forth out of my mouth: it shall not return unto me void, but it shall accomplish that which I please, and it shall prosper in the thing whereto I sent it."

The whiteness of the snow upon the soil is beautiful to see, but to know that beneath this blanket of white provision is being made for the next harvest that will sustain us in the coming season is divine! He cares for us ahead of tiem, and in this journey of life it has been good to know that just as seedtime and harvest has not failed, it is impossible that His Word towards me would ever fail that is found in Hebrews 1:2-3 ""2 Hath in these last days spoken unto us by his Son, whom he hath appointed heir of all things, by whom also he made the worlds; 3 Who being the brightness of his glory, and the express image of his person, and upholding all things by the word of his power, when he had by himself purged our sins, sat down on the right hand of the Majesty on high;…"

It is this relationship of covenant keeping that wherever we find ourselves at we know that God is never going to leave us or forsake those who belong to Him!

For those of you who are undecided about giving your life to Christ, why not give God a try – haven't you tried everything else imaginable by now? How has that worked out for you so far? Are you still lonely in the midst of a marriage, are you still dissatisfied in the midst of success, do you still need more than you needed the last time to get the same high off of the thrills and vices you use to sedate your mind?

Try God today and let Him take the rightful place that you have been filling with substitutionary living!

CHAPTER 10
Attitude and More Attitude

10- Attitude and More Attitude

Forbearance

Refraining from enforcement of something due Romans 2:4

Longsuffering

Long and patient endurance of offense Romans 9:22.

Meekness

Self-controlled, or slow to take offense, humble spirit, lowly in mind, and teachable. With a mildness, gentleness, usefulness, and a kindly disposition toward others. II Tim. 2:24, Titus 3:2, James 3:17, I Peter 2:18.

Quietness

secure by freeing from dispute or question. Job 34:29, Prov. 17:1, Is. 30:15

Peace

freedom from disquieting or oppressive thoughts or emotions. Ps. 37:37 and a state of repose and freedom from turmoil and agitation.

Patience

bearing pains or trials calmly or without complaint, manifesting forbearance under provocation or strain, steadfast despite opposition, difficulty or adversity. Luke 8:15, II Corinthians 6:4 and I Timothy 6:11.

Beatitudes

Lawson Hatfield states that the Beatitudes "Are the opening sentences of Jesus in the Sermon on the Mount which describe the quality of life of a citizen of the kingdom of God. The word "Beatitude" comes from a Latin word meaning "happy" or "blessed." Various forms of the word "bless" are used many times in both the Old and New Testaments, but this passage alone is known as the Beatitudes. The Sermon on the Mount (Matt. 5–7) sets forth the spiritual principles of the kingdom of God. They define the character of a child of the King. The Beatitudes are not to be seen as separate blessings for different believers. All the Beatitudes are to be applied and developed in all disciples both now and in the future." The eight Beatitudes have continuity. 1. "The poor in spirit" denotes the fact of sin (5:3). 2. "They that mourn" means to repent of sin (5:4). 3. "The meek" describes not the weak, but rather strength that is surrendered to God in a new birth experience (5:5). 4. To "hunger and thirst after righteousness" signifies the strong desire to become more Christ-like (5:6). 5. "The merciful" show an attitude of forgiveness (5:7). 6. "The pure in heart" strive daily for clean living (5:8). 7. "The peacemakers" exert a calming influence in the storms of life (5:9). 8. "They which are persecuted" denotes faithfulness under stress

(5:10-12). Each Beatitude carries with it a strong promise of ultimate good for those who develop the blessed life."

Peacemakers

Those who actively work to bring about peace and reconciliation where there is hatred and enmity. God blesses peacemakers and declares them to be His children (Matt. 5:9). Those who work for peace share in Christ's ministry of bringing peace and reconciliation (2 Cor. 5:18-19; Eph. 2:14-15; Col. 1:20).—Holman Bible Dictionary

Sons of God

Divine beings associated with God in the heavens in what can be called the "divine council" (Ps. 82:1 NRSV) or the "council of the holy ones" (Ps. 89:7 NAS). In Job, the earliest Greek translation translated "sons of God" as "angels of God" (Job 1:6; 2:1) and "my angels"

(Job 38:7). The phrase "sons of the living God" in Hosea 1:10, however, refers to Israel.

The expression sons of God employs a Hebrew idiom in which "son(s)" refers to participants in a class or in a state of being, and the second word describes the class or state of being. Thus, in Genesis 5:32, Noah is said to be a "son of five hundred years," meaning he was 500 years old. In English an adjective often best translates the second term, so that "divine beings" rather than "sons of God" would be a better rendition of the Hebrew. This accords with the NRSV's translation "heavenly beings" for "sons of gods" in Psalms 29:1; 89:6. In the New Testament, "sons of God" always refers to human beings who do God's will (Matt. 5:9; Rom. 8:14,19). Similar expressions with the same meaning are to be found in Matthew 5:45; John 1:12; Romans 9:26 (Hos. 1:10), and 2 Corinthians 6:18. The usual designation of the heavenly beings in the

New Testament is "angels." See Angel\n; Divine Council; God; Son of God.

Matthew Chapter 5

Christ begins His sermon on the mount:

1 And seeing the multitudes, he went up into a mountain: and when he was set, his disciples came unto him: 2 And he opened his mouth, and taught them, saying, declaring who are blessed

3 Blessed are the poor in spirit: for theirs is the kingdom of heaven. 4 Blessed are they that mourn: for they shall be comforted. 5 Blessed are the meek: for they shall inherit the earth. 6 Blessed are they which do hunger and thirst after righteousness: for they shall be filled. 7 Blessed are the merciful: for they shall obtain mercy. 8 Blessed are the pure in heart: for they shall see God. 9 Blessed are the peacemakers: for they shall be called the children of God. 10 Blessed are they which are persecuted for

righteousness' sake: for theirs is the kingdom of heaven. 11 Blessed are ye, when men shall revile you, and persecute you, and shall say all manner of evil against you falsely, for my sake. 12 Rejoice, and be exceeding glad: for great is your reward in heaven: for so persecuted they the prophets which were before you.

13 Ye are the salt of the earth: but if the salt have lost his savour, wherewith shall it be salted? it is thenceforth good for nothing, but to be cast out, and to be trodden under foot of men. 14 Ye are the light of the world. A city that is set on an hill cannot be hid. 15 Neither do men light a candle, and put it under a bushel, but on a candlestick; and it giveth light unto all that are in the house. 16 Let your light so shine before men, that they may see your good works, and glorify your Father which is in heaven.

17 Think not that I am come to destroy the law, or the prophets: I am not come to destroy,

but to fulfil. 18 For verily I say unto you, Till heaven and earth pass, one jot or one tittle shall in no wise pass from the law, till all be fulfilled. 19 Whosoever therefore shall break one of these least commandments, and shall teach men so, he shall be called the least in the kingdom of heaven: but whosoever shall do and teach them, the same shall be called great in the kingdom of heaven. 20 For I say unto you, That except your righteousness shall exceed the righteousness of the scribes and Pharisees, ye shall in no case enter into the kingdom of heaven.

21 Ye have heard that it was said by them of old time, Thou shalt not kill; and whosoever shall kill shall be in danger of the judgment: 22 But I say unto you, That whosoever is angry with his brother without a cause shall be in danger of the judgment: and whosoever shall say to his brother, Raca, shall be in danger of the council: but whosoever shall say, Thou fool, shall be in

danger of hell fire. 23 Therefore if thou bring thy gift to the altar, and there rememberest that thy brother hath ought against thee; 24 Leave there thy gift before the altar, and go thy way; first be reconciled to thy brother, and then come and offer thy gift. 25 Agree with thine adversary quickly, whiles thou art in the way with him; lest at any time the adversary deliver thee to the judge, and the judge deliver thee to the officer, and thou be cast into prison. 26 Verily I say unto thee, Thou shalt by no means come out thence, till thou hast paid the uttermost farthing.

27 Ye have heard that it was said by them of old time, Thou shalt not commit adultery: 28 But I say unto you, That whosoever looketh on a woman to lust after her hath committed adultery with her already in his heart. 29 And if thy right eye offend thee, pluck it out, and cast it from thee: for it is profitable for thee that one of thy members should perish, and not that thy whole

body should be cast into hell. 30 And if thy right hand offend thee, cut it off, and cast it from thee: for it is profitable for thee that one of thy members should perish, and not that thy whole body should be cast into hell. 31 , Whosoever shall put away his wife, let him give her a writing of divorcement: 32 But I say unto you, That whosoever shall put away his wife, saving for the cause of fornication, causeth her to commit adultery: and whosoever shall marry her that is divorced committeth adultery.

33 Again, ye have heard that it hath been said by them of old time, Thou shalt not forswear thyself, but shalt perform unto the Lord thine oaths: 34 But I say unto you, Swear not at all; neither by heaven; for it is God's throne: 35 Nor by the earth; for it is his footstool: neither by Jerusalem; for it is the city of the great King. 36 Neither shalt thou swear by thy head, because thou canst not make one hair white or black. 37

But let your communication be, Yea, yea; Nay, nay: for whatsoever is more than these cometh of evil.

He exhorts us to suffer wrong

38 Ye have heard that it hath been said, An eye for an eye, and a tooth for a tooth: 39 But I say unto you, That ye resist not evil: but whosoever shall smite thee on thy right cheek, turn to him the other also. 40 And if any man will sue thee at the law, and take away thy coat, let him have thy cloke also. 41 And whosoever shall compel thee to go a mile, go with him twain. 42 Give to him that asketh thee, and from him that would borrow of thee turn not thou away to love even our enemies

43 Ye have heard that it hath been said, Thou shalt love thy neighbour, and hate thine enemy. 44 But I say unto you, Love your enemies, bless them that curse you, do good to them that hate

you, and pray for them which despitefully use you, and persecute you; 45 That ye may be the children of your Father which is in heaven: for he maketh his sun to rise on the evil and on the good, and sendeth rain on the just and on the unjust. 46 For if ye love them which love you, what reward have ye? do not even the publicans the same? 47 And if ye salute your brethren only, what do ye more than others? do not even the publicans so? 48 Be ye therefore perfect, even as your Father which is in heaven is perfect.

Citizens of the Kingdom

Walking as citizens of the kingdom brings upon us the Aaronic Blessing found in Numbers 6:23-26 and the expanded understanding of that passage in the original text tells us that God the one who exists will kneel before us presenting gifts and will guard us with a hedge of protection; and will enlighten us towards being in order and not chaose, and will provide for us and set in our presence all we need to be whole and complete in Him.

He has given us the keys to the kingdom to possess and inhabit the land that he has set aside for us and to do it with an assurance that we are approved of when we walk in accordance to his word, and to do this we must walk in agreement as in Amos 3:3, Can two walk together, except they be agreed?

CHAPTER 11
A Fly In the Ointment

11- A Fly in the Ointment

This Chapter repeats for the sake of someone reading one volume and not the other. The importance of this chapter goes without saying, because "Sex" is the leading tool by which mankind is easily enticed and it is the practice of illicit sex and immoral performances that has driven the need for cures as we unabashedly refuse to restrain ourselves in the midst of horrific consequences!

A fly in the ointment brings forth a stinch that flows from us before God when we walk outside of the way of the Holy Spirit. When we walk after the spirit we will not fulfill the lust of the flesh and receive its consequences. We are reaping the dire consequences of lawlessness! The fly called (STDs), formerly known as venereal diseases, infectious diseases passed from one person to another primarily during sexual contact has come as a result of us not keeping exclusive to one well and one spring! When we use to visit the country and drink the well water, we were instructed to put the lid back on to keep it from being polluted and undrinkable. One well needs one lid! Are you keeping a lid on your well that God has given you ladies When a man comes to drop his bucket and draw refreshing water from you does he find a cool drink that is sweet like the well water in the countryside Or does he find water that has a stinch and is cloudy.

 Men are you dropping your bucket into the well where it has been laying around anywhere and not in its proper place hanging at the end of the rope that is attached to the reeling arm at the well. Or did you not bother to rewind the rope on the reel and just toss it down on the ground and let it roll around in the dirt, and let insects crawl inside and contaminate the bucket Have you let quenched anothers thirst from your ladle without washing it How responsible are you to the one God gave you and/or to the one God has promised you and to yourself This information bears repeating because far too many of us are killing ourselves with suicidal behavior in the name of pleasure! Too many innocent lives are lost because we want what we want and when we want it no matter who they belong to!

STDs are among the most common infections known—more than 12 million people in the United States, including 3 mililion teenagers, are infected with STDs every year. The United States has the highest STD rate in the industrialized world—roughly one in ten Americans will contract an STD during his or her lifetime.

Some STDs, such as or , may cause no symptoms.

People who do not know they are infected risk infecting their sexual partners and, in some cases, their unborn children. If left untreated, these diseases may cause debilitating pain or may destroy a woman's ability to have children. Some STDs can be cured with a single dose of antibiotics, but many, such as acquired immunodeficiency syndrome (AIDS), are incurable. People with these diseases remain infectious to others for their entire lives.

Those most at risk for contracting STDs are people who have unprotected sex—that is, sex without using a latex condom; those who have multiple partners; and those whose sex partners include intravenous drug users who share needles. Studies show that Americans between the ages of 16 and 24 are at greater risk for acquiring STDs than older adults are, because younger people are more likely to have multiple sexual partners rather than a single, long-term relationship. Additionally, young people may be more likely to have unprotected sex and may be embarrassed to tell their sexual partners they are infected. Young people may also be embarrassed or unable to seek treatment for STDs. This means that they are not only more likely to pass the disease to other young people, they also have a greater risk of suffering the long-term consequences of untreated STDs.

STDs are transmitted by infectious agents—microscopic bacteria, viruses, parasites, fungi, and single-celled organisms called protozoa—that thrive in warm, moist environments in the body, such as the genital area, mouth, and throat. Most STDs are spread during sexual intercourse (vaginal or anal), but other forms of sexual contact, such as oral sex, can also spread disease. Some STDs are passed from an infected mother to her child before birth, when the infection crosses the placenta and enters the baby's bloodstream; during childbirth, as the baby passes through the birth canal; or after birth, when the baby consumes infected breast milk.

Some viral STDs, especially AIDS, may be transmitted by blood. Such STDs may be passed between people who share infected needles or received through a transfusion of infected blood. Some people mistakenly believe that STDs can be transmitted through shaking hands or other casual contact, or through contact with inanimate objects such as clothing or toilet seats. Such transmissions are extremely rare.

Chlamydia

Chlamydia, caused by the Chlamydia trachomatis bacterium, is the most commonly transmitted STD in he United States. Because chlamydia may not produce noticeable symptoms, it often goes undiagnosed, and the CDC estimates that the true incidence of chlamydia is nearly ten times the number of reported cases.

People who do not know they are infected may not seek medical care and they may continue to have sex, unknowingly spreading the disease. When symptoms do develop, men may experience painful or burning urination or a discharge from the penis.

Women may experience burning urination, vaginal discharge, or mild lower abdominal pain. If left untreated, chlamydia damages reproductive tissue, causing inflammation of the urethra in men and possibly (PID) in women. PID can cause chronic, debilitating pelvic pain, infertility, or fatal pregnancy complications. Chlamydia infections are diagnosed by testing penile and vaginal discharge for the presence of the bacteria.

Gonorrhea

Gonorrhea, caused by the bacteria Neisseria gonorrhoeae, infects the membranes lining certain genital organs. Although roughly 356,000 gonorrhea infections are reported each year in the United States, experts estimate that closer to 800,000 people are infected annually. Like chlamydia, gonorrhea is often symptomless, and men are more likely to develop symptoms than women are. When present, symptoms may be similar to those of chlamydia and include burning urination and penile or vaginal discharge. Untreated gonorrhea can cause PID in women. Babies born to mothers with gonorrhea are at risk of infection during childbirth; such infections can cause eye disease in the newborn. Physicians diagnose gonorrhea by testing penile or vaginal discharge specimens for the presence of Neisseria gonorrhoeae. Gonorrhea is treatable with several antibiotics, although it has become resistant to treatment with many drugs in the past several decades.

Syphilis

Syphilis, a potentially life-threatening STD, is caused by the bacteria Treponema pallidum. According to the CDC, there are an estimated 38,000 new cases of syphilis in the United States each year. In the early stage of syphilis, a genital sore, called a chancre, develops shortly after infection and eventually disappears on its own. If the disease is not treated, the infection can progress over years, affecting the vertebrae, brain, and heart, and resulting in such varied disorders as lack of coordination, meningitis, and stroke. Syphilis is easily treated with penicillin, and the number of cases in the United States has dropped considerably since 1982. It is up to ten times more common in some regions of the southern United States than in other parts of the country. Syphilis during pregnancy can be devastating to the fetus, causing deformity and death, and most pregnant women in the United States receive screening for the disease in the first weeks of pregnancy so that the disease can be treated before the fetus is harmed.

Herpes

Genital Herpes is caused by infection with the herpes simplex virus (HSV). Most cases of genital herpes are due to HSV type 2. Some cases, however, result from genital infections with HSV type 1, a common cause of cold sores. Genital herpes causes recurrent outbreaks of painful sores on the genitals, although the disease often remains dormant with no symptoms for long periods. In the United States, one in five individuals over the age of 12 is infected with HSV type 2, and the vast majority of those infected—about 90 percent—do not know they have the disease. The symptoms of HSV can be treated with antiviral drugs, such as acyclovir, but HSV cannot be eradicated from the body—it is incurable.

AIDS, the result of infection with the (HIV), is an incurable and deadly STD. AIDS attacks the body's immune system, leaving victims open to a wide range of infections.

While HIV can be transmitted by other means, sex is the most common means of transmission. Women who are infected with HIV can pass the virus to their infants during childbirth or, less frequently, in breast milk. Treatment options for people infected with HIV include protease inhibitors, which can markedly increase survival. In spite of widespread educational and prevention programs, the CDC estimates that there are 46,000 new cases of HIV each year in the United States.

Certain types of hepatitis virus can be spread through sexual contact. One hundred times more contagious than HIV, hepatitis B is spread sexually and during childbirth: Between 90 and 95 percent of all babies born to infected mothers will contract the disease during birth. Hepatitis B attacks liver cells, leading to cirrhosis and possibly cancer of the liver. In most cases hepatitis B is incurable, but arduous chemotherapy can eliminate the virus in some patients. There is a safe, effective vaccination for hepatitis B, and most states are developing or already have initiated public school immunization programs.

Warts

Genital warts, transmitted by the during sexual contact, grow on the penis and in and around the entrance to the vagina and anus. The CDC estimates that there are 500,000 to 1 million new cases of genital warts in the United States each year. Although they are relatively painless, genital warts significantly increase the risk of cervical cancer in women. Genital warts are treatable with topical medications and can be removed with minor surgical procedures.

Trichomoniasis

Caused by infection with the protozoan Trichomonas vaginalis, causes vaginitis, inflammation of the vagina causing burning, itching, and discomfort. In men, trichomoniasis may cause similar problems in the urethra, called urethritis. Trichomoniasis is usually easily treated with a single dose of antibiotics. It is estimated that 5 million Americans are infected with trichomoniasis each year.

Unlike many serious diseases, STDs can be prevented by taking simple measures. The most effective prevention method is abstinence—that is, refraining from sex completely. No sexual contact means no risk of developing an STD. Practicing monogamy, in which two partners do not have sexual relations with anyone but each other, also greatly reduces the risk of spreading and contracting STDs.

Prevention of STDs

Latex are an effective, although not perfect, form of protection from STDs. These plastic sheaths, worn over the penis or inserted into the vagina, act as a physical barrier to organisms that cause STDs. However, condoms do not cover all of the genital surfaces that may come into contact during sex, and the possibility of transmission of some STDs, especially genital herpes and warts, still exists.

Early diagnosis and thorough treatment prevent the more serious consequences of infection, while halting the spread of STDs from person to person. This is most critical in STDs that do not cause symptoms, because those infected often do not know they risk infecting their sexual partners. Drug treatment programs must be completed, even if early doses of drugs appear to alleviate symptoms entirely. The infection may still persist in the absence of symptoms, leading infected individuals to unknowingly spread the disease. Furthermore, exposure to small doses of antibiotics that do not kill the infection may enable the infecting agent to develop resistance to the drug.

Screening

Public clinics screen patients at risk for STDs in order to diagnose and treat diseases in the early stages. Clinics track the incidence of STDs in particular areas and contact the sexual partners of infected individuals. By identifying and treating these potential carriers, clinics are able to break the chain of STD infections. Several organizations, such as the CDC and the World Health Organization, monitor and research the prevalence and transmission of STDs on an international level in an effort to prevent local outbreaks from reaching global, proportions. At any time in history, the prevalence and significance of different STDs mirror changes in science and society. For example, in many countries of the world, the incidence of STDs increased during and immediately after World War II (1939-1945), when soldiers spending extended periods of time away from home engaged in unprotected sexual relations with different partners, many of whom carried STDs. When the antibiotic penicillin became widely available in the following years, the same countries experienced dramatic reductions in STD incidence. Beginning in the 1950s, however, the incidence of gonorrhea began to rise as American sexual mores changed. Strains of the disease developed resistance to penicillin, and by the 1970s and 1980s the disease reached epidemic proportions in young adult populations.

Introduction of HIV into the human population led to an international crisis that began in the 1980s and continues to this day. Today record numbers of people are infected with genital herpes, and experts suspect that this incurable disease is quickly surpassing chlamydia as the most common STD in the United States.

Statistics:

Cases of STDs are increasing in the late 20th century, even though the use of condoms has increased since the onset of the AIDS epidemic. Public health officials feel that many factors are probably responsible, among them trends in sexual behavior. In the last several decades, the age at which people have sex for the first time has shifted downward, while the average number of partners a person has sex with during his or her lifetime has increased the risk of exposure to an STD.

My Dear Sisters and Brothers,

After becoming God conscious and aware of his ever presence as Jehovah Shammah, I began to renew my mind and lose my sin consciousness. Then he began to Sanctify me as Jehovah M'Kaddesh, with I Thessalonians 5:23; "And the very God of peace sanctify you wholly; and I pray God your whole spirit and soul and body be preserved blameless unto the coming of our Lord Jesus Christ." The he sealed me as El Shaddai, with Jude 1:24 "Now unto him that is able to keep you from falling, and to present you faultless before the presence of his glory with exceeding joy. To the only wise God our Savior, be glory and majesty, dominion and power, both now and ever. Amen" Seconds turned into minutes, minutes turned into hours and hours into days and days into months and months into years of his powerful presence, sanctification and might keeping me as I desire to be kept. Chaste and wholly His, until my earthly

Husband finds me! There is so much more that I want to tell you, but in the essence of space I must refrain. I will tell you this much, that I went through my life and recalled every name of every person that I had ever been with consentually and non-consentually, and went through a process of purification. I would be driving down the street and that person would come across my mind, I would take that name and myself before the throne of grace and receive mercy in my time of need. I would ask God to wash me, cleanse me, purify me and erase the very presence, the very odor of the person from me internally. I asked for a womb that would be a refreshing well spring to my future mate. I did this not once, but as often as Satan would push that rewind button. One day I knew I was making progress and getting stronger, because I would no longer think of that person and Satan would no longer push rewind, but hold on up would pop another name and face, and I would take them through the same process. It was like candy in a pez dispenser. Deal with that one and then the next one. Well all I know is that God is able to do exceeding and abundantly above what I could ask or think in my life. He delivered me from them and my self gratification! To God be the Glory! Trust Him, not me, Trust HIM, He is no respecter of persons, he will do the same for you. Take it a second at a time! How do you eat an elephant A bite at a time! This is a universal God, with a universal deliverance, this applies to both of you, male and female! You will find that the sacrifice of remaining chaste before God, rewarding you and your future mate!

Defiled No More

"Godly passion is reserved for the marriage bed. In the book of Genesis when God had completed some of his greatest works, he said "that it was good, and very good." Why do you think Satan makes you believe that what God ordained for you inside of marriage, is a necessity outside of marriage. Because he is the father of lies, I believe with all my heart, and knowledge of what God is, and desires for his people, is passion in every area of our lives. Many who have never been married in the natural to saved, born again, spirit-filled mates have yet to experience true passion.

The Song of Solomon is an awesome example of unconditional, holy passion. This passion describes God's love for his Church, by using a metaphor between a couple whom are on a journey of discovery.

The proper order of your sexuality is that a husband is to know a wife, and he enters into her and she receives him into herself. At the point of penetration the hymen ruptures, and blood is shed and a blood covenant is made between a husband and a wife. Her name has been kept in tact.

But if you think about how many people you have been with men and women, and how many of them are carrying your name spiritually it will shake you out of your slumber and easy ways.

The Hymen is a sheath that holds together the two walls of a woman's vagina. It is located at the base, the foundation the entrance into life, and into the world. As the blood co-mingles with the fluids of life a spiritual conversation is being spoken. It is also symbolic of a curtain, like the vail of the temple if you would, as it requires the shedding of blood to enter into the holy of holies.

This is worship people, pure worship! Saying, I am his, and he is mine – I vow to be your source of replenishing and bearer of your life, to honor you will all of my substance from the woman's part. The man is vowing to cover you at your weakest point, and to render to you the necessary source of life, to hold you close, and become the watchman on the wall. If you don't believe me, let's go to the word.

First, Song of Solomon 5:1-4, I AM come into my garden, my sister, my spouse: I have gathered my myrrh with my spice; I have eaten my honeycomb with my honey; I have drunk my wine with my milk; eat, O friends; drink, yea, drink abundantly, O beloved. I sleep, but my heart waketh: it is the voice of my beloved that knocketh, saying, Open to me, my sister, my love, my dove, my undefiled: for my head is filled with dew, and my fingers with sweet smelling myrrh, upon the handles of the lock." Song of Solomon 6:9 "My dove, my undefiled is but one; she is the only one of her mother, she is the choice one of her that bare her. The daughters saw her, and blessed her; year, the queens and the concubines, and they praised her."

Hebrews 13:4 "Marriage is honourable in all, and the bed undefiled: but whoremongers and adulterers God will judge." Remember it doesn't matter what is behind you, but before you. In Christ all things have become new, and old things have passed away. You have been restored no matter what anybody says. You start over at the point of salvation. If God designed you so meticulously and left not a single thing undone, surely he is able to restore your sexuality. After all he owns the patent on the original, surely he can restore what he has made. Jeremiah thought so, in chapter 18, verse 4. Whose report will you believe!

I shall believe the report of the Lord!...God has a plan for you and your sexuality to belong to him as his betrothed, so that you can go to a pure level of passion. That only comes from being intimate with him, through reading your word, praying, meditating, and talking to him. He said that he will keep those who desire to be kept, He is not a liar like those people who serve Satan you have been involved with.... Remember Don't Open that Door to fornication, Adultery, Immorality,

Let us put away childish behavior, and go in search of whom your soul loveth. Read I Corinthians 13:11 & Song of Solomon 3:1-3."

REMEMBER

"The female is the lock, and the male is the key. Apart from each other they don't fulfill the purpose of which they were designed. That is to secure those things, which are God given to them as a family ordained by God. A single born again woman has God as her key, and a single man has God as his lock. All things exist in Him! Don't open or be opened by just anyone!" Patricia E. Adams

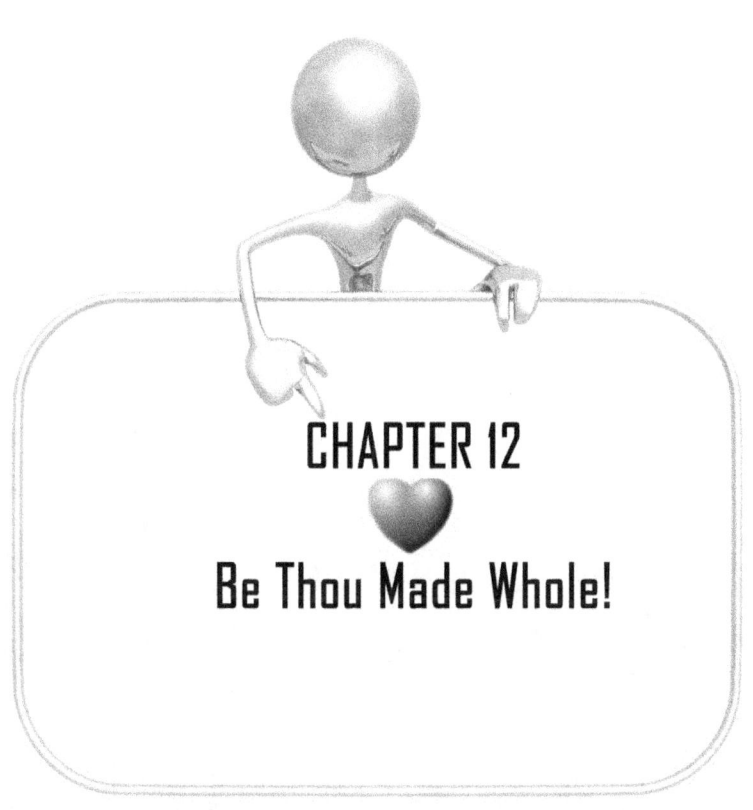

CHAPTER 12
Be Thou Made Whole!

12 – Be Thou Made Whole

When the people of Israel said, "All that G-d has spoken, we will do, and we will hear" (Exodus 24:7) -- giving precedence to "we will do" over "we will hear" -- a heavenly voice issued forth and exclaimed: "Who revealed to My children this secret, which is known only to the angels?"

There are 22 letters in the Jewish Alphabet and each of them are considered life within itself! Unlike our Alphabet system of 26 letter which have no literal authority assignment to them individually!

Sharing just a short sentence of what my understanding has garnered through my studies to see that when God did the creating it was truly finished! Where it had been broken due to fall – it has been thoroughly restored!

Letter 1 - Aleph:

Eternal God – Omnipotent; God's Oneness and Mastery.

Letter 2 - Beis:

At the Beginning, Blessing and Creator, Duality and Plurality.

Letter 3 - Gimmel:

Symbol of Kindness and Culmination.

Letter 4 - Dalet:

Symbol of Dimensions, Doors, Trust In.

Letter 5 - Hei:

Divinity, Gentility and Specificity, To Form.

Letter 6 - Vav:

Completion, Redemption and Transformation, Self-contained, Six Dimensions (Right & Left, Top and Bottom, Before and Behind).

Letter 7 - Zayin:

Spirit, Sustenance, Struggle, Purpose and comprised of the six physical directions: North and South, East and West, Up and Down, plus 1 for the Inner Man.

Letter 8 - Ches:

Transcendence, Divine Grace and Life.

Letter 9 - Tes:

Symbol of Goodness.

Letter 10 - Yud:
Creation, humility and indivisble God.

Letter 11 - Chof:
Crowning Accomplishment.

Letter 12 - Lamed:
Teaching and Purpose.

Letter 13 - Mem:
Revealed and Concealed (Moses and Messiah)

Letter 14 - Nun:
Faithfulness Soul nd Emergence.

Letter 15 - Samech:
Support and Protection and Memory.

Letter 16 - Ayin:
Sight and Insight.

Letter 17 - Peh:
Speech and Silence.

Letter 18 - Tzaddi:
Righteousness and Humility.

Letter 19 - Kuf:
Holiness and Growth Cycle.

Letter 20 - Reish:
Choosing Between Greatness or Degradation.

Letter 21 - Shin:
Divine Power and Script, also Corruption.
Letter 22 - Tav:
Truth and Perfection.

When God created the heavens and the earth according to John 1:1 ""IN THE beginning was the Word, and the Word was with God, and the Word was God. 1:2 "The same was in the beginning with God. 1:3 "All things were made by him, and without him was not any thing made that was made. 1:4 "In him was life; and the life was the light of men.""

When you reflect on the 22 letters above and see the weight of each them and it is from them that God spoke the universe and formed and created and made. Each letter having authority when needed to be combined with another to fulfill their purpose! Everything has a purpose under the sun and each of us are mean to fulfill that purpose in partnership!

My question to you is will though be made whole! The Word was with God in the beginning "at" the beginning and all things were created! Meaning the way of Escape the Door was present in Letter 4: Dalet: Symbol of Dimensions, Doors, Trust In.

Redemption and Deliverance and Healing and Wealth and Peace can all be seen reflected in the letters. Before the foundation of the earth "Patricia" put your name in " " I knew you before you were in your mothers belly and I called you by name before you were born to be full of purpose! To speak as in Letter 17: Peh: Speech and Silence. To have witty ideas, concepts, innovations as in Letter 16: Ayin: Sight and Insight. We could go on and on with this! But the point I am making at the end of Volume 3 "Detouring **off** the Road Called Oneness" is because God says it is TIME TO MANIFEST!

Wherever you are, whomever you are blaming for your lack of success or happiness! Today is the day that you harden not your heart! If you have been backslidden because the church is full of hypocrisy, come on home anyway! You are not there for the people but for God! So, come be listed as those whose robes have been washed in the Blood of the Lamb! God already knows whose for Him; whether in the church or outside of the Church! That really is none of your business! Your Business is to Manifest in your Space – not someone elses!

Again, who hinders you now that you do not run this race! Take a look in the mirror – you might find the answer! No matter how difficult the situation may seem, choices got us in and choices have to get us out! We are right where we are because we chose to be there as adults! For the children some of you are where you are until you are emancipated! No worries – God took that into consideration too! There is a way of Escape for all of us – or God has lied! And His Word is SETTLED in HEAVEN FOREVER! So, the circumstances surrounding you must be lying to you – by telling you that you cannot get up and you cannot get out and you will never amount to anything! You are a third generation failure the Devil is telling you! Are you dead, pinch yourself; did you feel any pain? As long as you are breathing and can feel that pinch you have an opportunity to do what God designed you to do, what ONLY YOU were created to DO! Once more who hinders that you do not run!

Endnotes

MATERIALS
Bibles: King James Version

Books:
Myles Munroe, copyright 1991
Single, Married, Separated & Life After Divorce
Bahamas Faith Ministries Published by Vincom, Inc.
P.O. Box 702400
Tulsa, OK 74170
Reprint Permission Granted by Vincom, Inc.

Eugenia Price
Woman to Woman, copyright 1959
Zondervan Books
Zondervan Publishing House
Grand Rapids, MI 49506
Used by Permission of Zondervan Publishing House

Derek and Ruth Prince
God Is A Matchmaker, 1986
Chosen Books a Division of Baker Book House
P.O. Box 6287
Grand Rapids, MI 49516-6287
Used by Permission of Baker Book House

Spiros Zodhiates
The Complete Word Study – New Testament
Chattanooga, TN 37422
AMG Publishers, 1991
6815 Shallowford Rd.
Box 22000
Reprint Permission Granted by AMG Publishers

Volumes in the One Heart Series

VOLUME 1
With Oneness of Heart: Preparing to Regain My Original Position in Life
ISBN 0-9700976-0-3
Formats: Paper, Audio, E-Book & Digital, Kindle

VOLUME 2
Book: Journeying to the Road Called Oneness: To Regain My Original Position in Life
ISBN 0-9700976-1-1
Formats: Paper, Audio, E-Book & Digital, Kindle

VOLUME 3
Detouring off the Road of Oneness: Away from My Original Position in Life
ISBN 0-9700976-2-X
Formats: Paper, Audio, E-Book & Digital, Kindle
Book: Disciple's Guide
Audio: Disciple's Overview

VOLUME 4
I and My Father Are One: Abiding in My Regained Position
ISBN 0-9700976-3-8
Formats: Paper, Audio, E-Book & Digital, Kindle
Book: Disciple's Guide
Audio: Disciple's Overview

VOLUME 5
One Heart Series Devotional 52 Weeks: Sustaining My Regained Position in Life
ISBN 09700976-7-0
Formats: Paperback

Other Books by Patricia E. Adams cont'd

Set Free to Praise Him: A Childs' Rights Violated
"Her Terrors and Traumas"
ISBN 0-9700976-5-4

Salvation "Soteria" Unpack It and Use It, It's More Than a Ticket To Heaven ,
 ISBN 0-9700976-4-6

Shortcuts Consequences Integrity on the Line: Will You Take the Low Road or the High Road
ISBN 0-9700976-6-2

Help My Fears Shadow is Chasing Me (PTSD) Traumas Aftershock
ISBN 0-9700976-8-9

Fiery Darts of the Assassin: Know the Nature of the Enemy Satan
ISBN 0-9700976-9-7

www.ingramcontent.com/pod-product-compliance
Lightning Source LLC
Chambersburg PA
CBHW070335240426
43665CB00045B/1988